Outposts

and

Bushplanes

Bruce Lamb

hancock

house

ISBN 0-88839-556-6

Cataloging in Publication Data

Lamb, Bruce
    Outposts and bushplanes / Bruce Lamb.

Includes bibliographical references and index.
ISBN 0-88839-556-6

    1. Lamb, Bruce, 1925– 2. Bush pilots—British Columbia,
Northern—Biography. 3. British Columbia, Northern—Biography. 4. Prince
George Region (B.C.)—Biography. 5. British Columbia, Northern—History.
I. Title.

FC3845.N67Z49 2005   971.1'8204'092   C2004-905855-X

Printed in South Korea — PACOM

Editor: Nancy Miller
Production: Ingrid Luters
Front cover design: Rick Groenheyde

Front cover photo: Quiet solitude of an Omineca area lake.
Back cover photos: *From top*, Mountain view; Examining the shovel used to replace the tail ski, before
the aircraft went through the ice, photo by Milt Warren; Junkers 34 CF-ATF; The HBC post at Takla
Landing; author Bruce Lamb.
Page 128: Moose, photo by David Hancock.
All photographs © Bruce Lamb unless otherwise credited.

*We acknowledge the financial support of the Government of Canada through the
Book Publishing Industry Development Program (BPIDP) for our publishing activities.*

Published simultaneously in Canada and the United States by

HANCOCK HOUSE PUBLISHERS LTD.
19313 Zero Avenue, Surrey, B.C. V3S 9R9
(604) 538-1114 Fax (604) 538-2262

HANCOCK HOUSE PUBLISHERS
1431 Harrison Avenue, Blaine, WA 98230-5005
(604) 538-1114 Fax (604) 538-2262
Web Site: www.hancockhouse.com *email:* sales@hancockhouse.com

Contents

To our grandsons and granddaughters —
Jody and Danny Lamb, Jesse and Megan Lamb

Preface

This book was written as a celebration of the fine people who populated the great hinterlands, relishing its splendor and independence. While I was gathering material for this story, it was plainly and painfully obvious that so many people I had known, who could have given me no end of information, had passed on. This increased my determination to continue with the story, trying to preserve history from those of us who still remember and hoping to give a young generation a true account of what things were like in the middle of the century just passed. Maybe, also, I would be able to create a better understanding of what the people of that age were like and how they fit into the lifestyles of the times.

In the 1980s, about twenty years after having left Prince George, I was visiting that city. Alf Janke, the veteran game warden, had been gone about the same length of time but happened to be in Prince George the same day and, incredibly, we saw each other. I was in a crowded Woodward's store when I heard a booming voice call out, "Bruce." I turned and there was Alf, extending his hand. His first words were, "You're the second old-timer I've met today!" That made me feel good to think such a legendary old veteran of the times as Alf Janke would immediately look upon me as an "old-timer!" Maybe I really did belong to that long-past, fabulous period of time that knew boundless freedoms, real wilderness and endless adventures with true and lasting friendships.

I sincerely wish to thank all the people who helped me in various ways while writing this story. First, a big thanks to Milt Warren for making all those morning fires and cooking my breakfasts while I lay in my warm, down sleeping bag! But I still played jokes on him, as he did to me. One time in late winter we were having our noon lunch on the sunny side of a hill where most of the snow had melted. We were sitting beside and above our fire, while between us was a poplar pole about the diameter of a man's arm. We had two buns left and these were lying on the little log above the fire. I moved, accidentally bumping the pole, and one bun rolled down and into the coals of the fire. I quickly said, "Milt, your bun rolled into the fire!" Milt grabbed it out, blew ashes from it and said, "It's okay, I can still eat it." I could hardly keep a straight face, but I did, and we carried on our activities. That night we had been to bed for maybe fifteen minutes, when Milt suddenly raised his head from his sleeping bag and loudly exclaimed, "How the hell come that was my bun that rolled in the fire?" That's when I really roared out laughing as Milt had just then realized he had been had.

Milt was a great help as I wrote this story. I would send him drafts, and he would help me out with names I had forgotten, or retell an incident he had probably told me years ago as we sat around some cozy campfire in the wilderness. The times I write about were so different from what they are now and Milt fully agreed with me that the story should be told in order to try to preserve a bit of history.

Many thanks are due to Marge Donovan, the "Little Marge," of old Finlay Forks. I also sent her a draft of the part of the story relating to Finlay Forks, asking her to pick it apart to see if there were any problems. Marge helped to fill me in on various little events and was no end of help with names and dates. She also came through by giving me access to a large number of photos from her grandparents' collection for use in the story, a great contribution to be sure.

Another old-time family who helped me out was the Pan Phillips clan, formerly of the upper Blackwater. By this time both Pan and his wife had passed on, but I contacted Ken, their eldest son, sending him a draft of the chapter regarding his family and the Blackwater country. Ken's wife wrote a nice letter to me correcting some of my dates and happenings. This was greatly appreciated because it gives a certainty to the story.

Many thanks to Bob Darnall for letting me use pictures of him to help illustrate the story. Also, many thanks to Bob for the great times we spent together, often in some beautiful wilderness or mountain location far away from any human habitation or road, including one outing when bad weather prevented our getting back on time, causing some concern.

Two of our friends had a cabin at Azouzetta Lake in the Pine Pass, where a few people would often gather for a weekend in winter and spring and ski on the mountains. This was long before there was any ski facilities at Pine Pass, so we would put "skins" on our skis and climb to the top of the mountains, then ski down. During one of the enjoyable evenings spent in the warm cabin heated by a big woodstove one of us, it may have been me, came up with a novel idea. Why not add some zest to the skiing by towing someone behind the aircraft on a frozen lake with the aircraft in flight?

Bob Darnall quickly agreed to be the one towed and plans were swiftly made. On a Sunday afternoon Bob and I flew to McLeod Lake, while some other people drove up to watch. We tied a long, light rope to the rear of the aircraft; Bob got on his skis and held onto the other end. I taxied out to tighten the rope, then applied take-off power. When the airplane became airborne I kept it just feet above the lake as we flew along. I could not see back, so I had no way of knowing how Bob was doing. Suddenly, a snowshoe trail showed up at an angle to our line of flight. I thought this might cause trouble for Bob on his skis, so I quickly landed. Much to my relief he came sliding up beside the aircraft before we were even stopped, as he glided on the snow better than did the airplane! When Bob told his version of the story he said he hadn't seen the snowshoe trail, but something had given him a big bump and launched him into the air! He said he thought for a while he was going to take off!

One of the people who came to watch us was a friend who happened to be a professional photographer. He got a picture of us in flight and had it published in the *Prince George Citizen*. The caption stated it was the first time this had ever been done in Canada. Maybe we started this thing they call extreme sports, who knows!

My greatest hope is that people will get as much enjoyment from reading this story as I did in writing it. It was a pleasant excuse to contact someone I hadn't seen in years in order to get verification on something, often names and spellings. When I went through my collection of old pictures I couldn't understand why I had not taken more. In my mind I can see so many things I would love to have had a picture of but just didn't think of it at the time. However, I hope readers enjoy the pictures that I did manage to take.

CHAPTER 1

People of the Trench

hen the dam on the Peace River at Hudson's Hope was constructed in the mid-1960s, it flooded an absolutely fabulous area. A huge block of land below the dam site, extending far into Alberta, was well known as the famous "Peace River block." The vast region upstream from the site of the dam was simply called "the Upper Peace." This was the area the officers of the Northwest Company traveled through when they established the first white settlement in British Columbia west of the Rocky Mountains. Built on a far-away tributary of the Peace, this historic post was named Fort McLeod. What the establishers of the post found was a great inland empire, all connected by waterways. A land of rugged mountains, many with icy summer caps, thousands of creeks and streams with sparkling clear water, green forests and hundreds of miles of flat valley bottoms all linked by rivers.

This large network of rivers that provided tremendous access to such a huge and unique area had a strange quirk. Once into this great land there were hundreds of miles of relatively quiet water on the rivers, allowing easy navigation by small boats. But on every major river giving access to the area, except one, there was a wicked canyon or gorge. Was this Mother Nature's way of only grudgingly allowing people to see her intricate handiwork? Was it to further test their mettle by forcing them to first get past a formidable river canyon?

Nevertheless, hardy adventurous souls were not long in coming to the region to harvest the wild fur from the bush and the alluvial gold from the river bars. Others spent a near lifetime scouring the hills, picking at rocks, blasting and digging holes, determined to find the illusive rich mineral deposits they were so certain that nature must have hidden somewhere deep in the wilderness. And right along with the trappers and the prospectors came the people who would create the trading posts to accommodate them.

Besides the Upper Peace, the Lower Finlay and Lower Parsnip, the main valleys drowned, the dam flooded the lower reaches of no less than eleven other waterways designated as rivers. One beautiful stream, about thirty feet wide and well known locally for its excellent trout and grayling fishing, the Carbon, was just registered as a "creek." I can attest to the excellent fishing quality of the pretty stream.

In the late 1950s I had the job of flying an aircraft belonging to Industrial Forestry Service Ltd. in Prince George. I flew B.C. Registered Foresters and their crews to mostly remote lakes and rivers throughout much of northcentral British Columbia. They were doing inventory work on available timber, as well as preliminary work on road locations that have since developed into a great network of forestry roads. We landed on rivers and lakes with floats in the summer and on the frozen waterways on skis in the winter. One of the principals in the company was Bob Darnall. His folks, old-timers from the Fort St. John area, had two cabins on a bench near the mouth of Carbon Creek.

This was a popular resort spot for Peace River people, thus there was also a well-used camping area among the tall, great, canopied cottonwood trees. This was a once-permanent trading post, complete with a post office bearing the tantalizing name Gold Bar. Over the September long weekend it was a ritual for a group of people from Fort St. John to gather at the Carbon. There is no better time than this to be in the outdoors in northcentral B.C., and these people would tell you there was no finer place to be than the Peace River at the mouth of Carbon Creek.

For at least two different years, Bob asked me if I would fly him there, stay with them in one of their cabins, then fly him back to Prince George on the Monday evening. The plan called for me to forgo my regular, rather generous, flying pay and just go for the trip. No arm twisting was required to make it a deal, but the first year there was a catch. These people were all fly fishermen and Bob said

I would be laughed out of existence if I showed up with my spinning outfit. I had never fished with a fly rod before, but I borrowed an appropriate outfit, got some flies along with five minutes of instructions and then we were away.

Bright and early the next morning Bob, his brother and I started up the Carbon. They said that further up the river was better fishing, so we walked two miles before we wet a fly. I soon had quite a variety on my catch list—such diverse articles as my hat, willows, rocks and a fine specimen of a spruce tree. However, before the day was out I lost track of how many fat, solid, fighting trout and colorful arctic grayling I had caught and released from the clear, cold water of Carbon Creek. This beautiful mountain stream certainly lived up to its reputation.

Mother Nature went all out in forming her obstacle to access of the Upper Peace from the east. She constructed an exceptionally wicked gorge fourteen miles long that became known as the Peace River Canyon. I have flown just above the rim of the entire gorge, staring at the formidable scene below. I can't find words to properly describe the terrifying way the water would pour through a narrow shoot, then smash against a solid rock wall, sending water and mist high into the air. Equally awesome were the vicious whirlpools, the speed of the water and the constant crashing of it against rock walls. Common opinion was that the canyon had never been navigated by boat. But the history books tell us that in 1828 a crew of rivermen of Chief Factor McDonald of the Hudson's Bay Company actually made it up the gorge, in very low water, in a large canoe with the men doing lots of lining. (Lining was achieved by having men on shore or rock shelves pull the canoe along, while a man or two stayed in the canoe and guided it through the water by means of a long pole.)

Even though the HBC's rivermen made the trip, normal access to the Upper Peace from the east was by way of a portage road around the canyon, then by riverboat. A minor rapid, more like two or three little rock shelves extending most of the way across the river and named the Ne Parle Pas, was located about forty miles farther up the river. There was one more set of rapids just short of the junction of the Parsnip and Finlay, the two rivers that together formed the Peace River proper. These rapids were more a boulder-strewn, wider stretch of mostly shallow and fast water that created a roar heard for miles. Experienced rivermen took either of these two rapids in stride without giving them a second thought.

From early fur-trading days a supply post of sorts operated intermittently at the junction of the Parsnip and Finlay. From HBC records, it appears they had a store there in 1824. After World War One the post at the junction, then operated independently, was given the services of a government wireless communication station with an operator. In 1925 a trading post was established about four miles up the Finlay on the west side on a large, flat bench near the head of Pete Toy's Bar. This long gravel bar in the river that gave the new trading post sheltered moorage in all but very high water, was named after the prospector who had earlier taken a small fortune in gold from it.

In 1926 the owner of the new post left for a period of time, so he arranged for Roy MacDougall to operate it in his absence. However, the owner of the post never returned and Roy MacDougall stayed on. The old settlement at the junction of the two rivers faded away, while the new post lived on, receiving a post office with the name Finlay Forks. The government wireless communication station was moved there and at one time a B.C. game warden was stationed at the new Finlay Forks. The MacDougalls operated the post continuously, right up to the time they were bought out when the area was flooded.

This area is part of the great Rocky Mountain Trench that runs on the west side of the Rockies from Montana north-northwest to the Yukon. Finlay Forks was near the center of the very distinctive northern section. The Peace River is unique in that it is the only river between the Northwest Territories and New Mexico that flows east, straight through the Rocky Mountains!

The earliest explorers made their way from Finlay Forks up the Parsnip to the Pack River, which took them to McLeod Lake, then up the Crooked River to Summit Lake. This southerly route was the only entrance into the area not obstructed by a major river canyon. From Summit Lake early travelers could traverse a portage of only about ten miles to get to the Fraser River, crossing from the Arctic to the Pacific watershed. In the late 1920s, a road of sorts was built from Prince George to Summit Lake, a distance of about thirty miles. River travelers to the north could then easily start from Summit Lake though the outlet, Crooked River, was only a twisting creek first with shallows and rocks, later becoming slow moving, wider and deeper except for some chutes.

A rather large river, the Omineca, coming from the west joined the Finlay a few miles north of Finlay Forks. This river provided excellent navigation for boats from the west for something like 130 miles. But before the Finlay was reached, one had to get past the wild gorge, known as either Pete Toy's Canyon or Black Canyon. The name Black was not given because of color or shade; it was named after an early explorer of that name. It also was known as Pete Toy's Canyon in memory of the hardy prospector of that name who was drowned in it. This canyon was second only to the Peace River Canyon in ferocity. A tributary, the Mesilinka, had navigable water once one was past Dog Canyon, near its junction with the Omineca.

The Nation River system afforded limited access from the southwest, but it had a bad canyon. From the northwest came the Ingenika, entering the Finlay north of Fort Graham. It, too, had a bad gorge, but otherwise provided quite a bit of navigable water. Its tributaries, the Swannell and the Pelly, added many more miles of water access. Dick Corless, the dean of the river freighters, soon to be introduced to this narrative, used to take freight a considerable distance up all these tributary rivers for the trappers. He also took in mountain hunters.

A riverboat service to the trading posts and others in the trench started prior to 1930, with Summit Lake as the southern terminus. Dick Corless from Prince George worked on it and then purchased the outfit in 1931. He operated a fleet of boats on the rivers, right up to the time they were flooded by the dam. For many years a second commercial riverboat service was operated by Art Van Somer. Their boats were more than forty feet long with pointed nose and wide, flat bottoms with a slight slope up at both front and rear. They were made from spruce boards; the rivermen themselves built new boats during the winter months. Powered by one Johnson outboard motor of either twenty-two or twenty-five horsepower, they could haul more than six tons to a load. The boats were completely open, so perishable freight had to be covered by a well-tied tarp for protection from the weather.

Two men operated each boat. One stayed at the rear to run the motor, or "kicker" as they were known, while the other man stayed in the bow with a paddle and a pike-pole. The bowman would use his equipment to help control the boat in difficult water, as well as to "read the water," including measuring the depth of the water with his pole. This was particularly important in the silty water of the Finlay, and some others, where the bottom couldn't be seen. Among the items of spare equipment they carried was an extra outboard motor.

From Summit Lake the boats had to be only partially loaded until deeper water was reached further down the Crooked River. Thus, two or three relay trips would be required for each load. A round trip to Fort Ware could take well over a month. In 1952 the gravel-surfaced Hart Highway, passing close to McLeod Lake, was completed to Dawson Creek, so river travel could then start at Fort McLeod. Without the shallow, small and twisting little Crooked River to navigate, they not only saved time and work, but could now use larger boats and haul heavier loads.

My means of travel "up the trench," was by air, beginning in 1953. After leaving Fort McLeod the aircraft was headed for Finlay Forks, and eight minutes later when the dusty Hart Highway (now Highway 97) faded from sight under the right wing, all evidence of mechanized man was gone! From there on the Rocky Mountain Trench was completely devoid of roads, air strips, mines, logging or any other activity involving machines, right through to the Alaska Highway. The only exception was a small sawmill, which at one time had been set up at Finlay Forks. This was a huge land, sparingly settled by hardy, neighborly people in a large, close-knit society. It was a land of riverboat travel in the summer and dog teams by winter, with bush planes occasionally dropping by either winter or summer. It was a land of endless freedoms and independence, virtues so deeply cherished by the people living on the banks of its beautiful rivers and among the scenic mountains.

There was so much history in that country. And so much drama, some of it of life or death severity, while other events just made great stories to be told and retold in warm log cabins on cold winter nights or around evening campfires deep in the wilderness. The following incident fits the latter category.

Lou Strandberg had a trapline in the Finlay Forks area. Having more than one cabin, he would be away from a cabin for a few days at a time. One very cold January late afternoon, he returned to one of his cabins after dark and was surprised to find the door open. Walking into the cold, dark hut to get a candle for some light, he bumped into something big, furry and hard. Even in the dark he knew the place was a mess, but when he finally found candles to get a light going he was shocked to see not only that his cabin was indeed a shambles, but a large, frozen grizzly bear was actually lying stretched out on his bunk! Grizzly bears will, the odd time, come out of hibernation in the dead of winter—and when they do, they are hungry. This bear had eaten everything in sight in the cabin, including a full can of baking powder, which has been credited with killing him.

Lou had an awful night in the approximately minus forty-degree temperature. He had to get that heavy, stiff bear off his bunk and outside before he could even get a fire going, then start clean-up.

I had heard this tale from several sources, but in more recent years, after Lou was gone, I asked his wife to again tell me the frozen bear story. Ida, a sister of Dick Corless, spent her last few years near the town where I live in southern B.C. She enjoyed coming into the office where I worked to visit; she said I was the only one she could talk with about the north. The day she refreshed my memory of the frozen bear was the last time I saw her before she, too, suddenly passed away. And, oh, how many more stories of the north were gone forever?

As one flew above the Parsnip River heading north a large cabin with an upstairs, very elaborate for the bush, would come into view across the river from the mouth of Scotts Creek. That cabin itself was shrouded in mystery and intrigue. Located on a long, straight stretch of the river, it had observation ports in the gable ends, allowing anyone approaching on the river to be observed well before they arrived. It was built in 1912 by a man named Scott, who, it was rumored, had to leave Montana in a hurry because he had killed a man. Before long, Scott was feuding with a trapper named Weston, who lived about thirteen miles further north, near a creek named for him. Weston left a note in his cabin one winter day saying he was going to Scott's place and "…if I don't come back, you'll know where to look for me." He never came back, nor was his body ever found!

In 1949 this cabin, six smaller "line cabins" and the huge trapline that went with them, were purchased by Milt Warren and his brother, Bob. The Warrens came from Geraldton, Ontario. As a young man, Milt joined the RCAF, completing a full tour of duty in bomber command as a wireless airgunner, for which King George VI personally pinned a medal on his chest. Before getting the trapline, he, along with his dad and brothers, had operated quite a large hydraulic gold mining operation on Germansen River. In 1952 Milt got married, sold the trapline, then joined the B.C. Game Department in their newly established predator control branch. Milt Warren was definitely among those who knew the area of the Rocky Mountain Trench country and its people most thoroughly.

Over a period of about the next ten years Milt Warren and I went on more trips together than either of us could ever remember. We used a Jeep pick-up to get to hunting areas, then we sometimes used horses but often went on back-packing trips, usually into some mountain range. We prospected together, sometimes on trips involving flights into very remote areas in the winter time, where we would camp in a tent with a fire out front for cooking and sitting around while we told stories. Sometimes I flew him on his official government work. Today, in British Columbia, it is impossible to get as far from any road as were some of the wild and beautiful valleys at the time we left the ashes from our campfires and the tracks from our snowshoes in them.

There are some things I remember very well about all our trips together. During all our camping together on all of those trips, Milt made the morning fire and cooked breakfast every single time! In the dead of winter he would roll out of his big warm, down sleeping bag with his long wool underwear and socks on, slip into his shoes, then make the fire. He would cook breakfast, but not until after we had finished eating would he get dressed! And remember, all of this happened outside the tent around a campfire, often on the packed snow in a frozen north! I usually didn't get up until that wonderful aroma of coffee brewing in a campfire-blackened tin pail over the glowing coals permeated the cold morning air. But I guess I must have done something right to get all that service, because on all our trips together we never had a single word of disagreement.

As mentioned, the large trapline owned by Milt Warren and his brother was eventually sold. The buyer was a trapper named Roland Skog. One time he failed to show up when he should have, so a search was started. Roland was found outside one of the line cabins;

he had been killed by a bear. At that time in history bears had a great fear of man and attacks on people were very rare. Thus, it was extremely unusual to find that the man had been killed by a bear, especially right beside his cabin. It was not determined whether it had been a black bear or a grizzly. But the trapper was in his night attire! This would indicate he went out of the cabin at night, probably to have a pee, when he stumbled onto, maybe right into, a very surprised bear, which quickly killed him.

Continuing the trip north, the Finlay River, with its silty-colored water, appears from the north. It meets the clear water of the Parsnip from the south. Together now, they turn east, circle north, then head straight east. This happened right at the foot of spectacular Mount Selwyn, which stood as a great, silent guard watching over the mixing of two historical waterways, as together they made up the beginning of the mighty Peace River. Four miles farther north we circle over the buildings of the trading post of Finlay Forks. We check the wind and look for driftwood in the river, then come in for a landing on the smooth, straight stretch of the Finlay and taxi into the dock. Roy MacDougall will already be there to help with tying up the aircraft.

Finlay Forks was by far the finest of the three trading posts that once graced the Finlay River. Built on a nice, level bench, the trading post with post office was in a separate building from the house, both neatly built of logs with some lumber add-on rooms on the house. All buildings were spread out, connected by cute paths and little fields. By the time I appeared on the scene, the wireless station and the game warden's house were just vacant buildings. With the departure of the government communication radio station some years previous, the entire Rocky Mountain Trench area was left without any type of electronic communication. But what set Finlay Forks apart from the other trading posts was the feminine touch, embodied by Roy's wife, Marge. They had a granddaughter whom they called "Margie," but everyone else referred to her as "Little Marge." Little Marge spent her early years at Finlay Forks, then later she came for all of every summer holiday until the post was closed by the flooding.

I used to look at her and think what a great place it was for a girl to spend her holidays. It was so wonderfully quiet and serene, with the Finlay River flowing smoothly by, the great Mt. Selwyn staring down at them from across the river and on a still summer evening one could hear the distant roar of the Finlay Rapids just below the junction on the Peace River. And it was isolated. In the fall of the year there would be at least two months without contact from the outside, until nearly Christmas time when ice would be thick enough to land aircraft on. Some people may think this would be lonely and desolate, but the occupants of this post certainly didn't think so!

It was the remoteness of the area, completely devoid of land access, other than the river, that made it so attractive. Road access, with the masses flocking in, plunks all areas into the same melting pot, and no area with a road connection can be considered really unique from any other place. At the time I knew the Rocky Mountain Trench almost no adventurous visitors ever came in by their own boat, just for the trip and to see the country, or to fish for fighting trout or the beautiful grayling that frequented so many clear streams emptying into the Parsnip and the Finlay. "Little" Marge Donovan has recently told me that she never knew of anyone coming in his own boat from the south just for the trip! She said a very few came up the Peace River from Hudson's Hope. R. M. (Raymond) Patterson, author of several books, traveled the south route on tours in his canoe, largely to gather material for books. A doctor from Dawson Creek used to holiday for two or three weeks every summer all by himself somewhere up the Finlay River or its tributaries. He would come up the Peace, starting of course above the portage, traveling in a good-sized Peterborough freight canoe. These very efficient craft were constructed with light, thin wooden narrow planks over wood ribs, then covered with canvas, just as most canoes of yore were made. Only the freight models had nearly flat, rounded bottoms and a square stern. It took only a very small outboard motor to drive them up rivers, even with a considerable load. I never saw the doctor up there, but I had been at Finlay Forks when the MacDougall's said he was somewhere up-river.

Of course, Marge and Roy were delighted to have their granddaughter with them in the summer and it was easy to see they simply doted on her. One time I landed at Finlay Forks about 2:00 in the afternoon to fuel up, then carry on. Marge was away and Roy, Little Marge and her mother, Florence, were there. They asked me to come in and have lunch, but meal time was over and I didn't want to bother them. But Florence insisted I needed something to eat, and it was not easy to leave the MacDougall's without first eating! So we went to the house and Florence made me a very delicious sandwich, along with fresh coffee. When Roy and I returned to the dock, Little Marge was sitting in the pilot's seat, "flying" my aircraft. Roy looked at her, then with a deep voice that was supposed to sound tough, but was actually dripping with affection, said, "Margie, get out of there." He couldn't quite hide the little grin that slid across his face!

Most of the people in the isolated north were of splendid character, but the MacDougalls were outstanding. Marge had a long serving table on the edge of her kitchen and every traveler that came along sat at it and ate. And she never charged anyone for a meal. When Milt Warren was trapping he said that as many as twelve trappers would come and have Christmas with the MacDougalls! However, while the trappers were there for Christmas they would cut and split enough firewood to last the MacDougalls a full year, until the next Christmas. Roy had horses and before Christmas he would skid in a bunch of dry logs for the trappers to saw into firewood. When I talked to Roy about his horses, he said each was over twenty years old and they had never been in a barn! Finlay Forks was in a light snowfall area and the horses pawed through the snow for most, if not all, of their feed. What a wonderful country it was before the human dam builders discovered it!

I have experienced firsthand just how thoughtful and caring were the MacDougalls. One winter day Milt and I were flying north. We went over Finlay Forks a thousand feet in the air and made no effort whatsoever at recognition. We didn't waggle the wings or change engine speed—nothing. Several days later on our way south we landed at Finlay Forks. When we stepped inside the house Marge looked at me and said, "Where have you been? We were worried about you, we saw you go over last Tuesday and thought you would be back to spend the night with us. Then, when you didn't come the next day, we got real worried!" They had recognized the aircraft I flew and were looking out for us. What terrific people.

But the great benevolence and popularity of Marge didn't prevent her from bearing the brunt of the oldest trick in the trapping trade. Some black, domestic house cats, with a pelt worth nothing, look very similar to a female fisher, which is one of the higher-priced furs on the market. Since time immemorial an inexperienced fur buyer in the hinterlands has been sold the hide of a hapless tom-cat, the trapper saying it is a fisher.

While Marge was still an inexperienced fur buyer and Roy was away, a trapper brought in some fur, which she purchased. Among the pelts was this nice "fisher"! This happened twenty some years before I was in the country, but I still heard the story from more than one source, how old so-and-so (I forget the trapper's name) sold a tom-cat to Marge MacDougall! This really went the rounds on the "moccasin telegraph," and poor Marge couldn't begin to remember how many people had come in and asked her if she had bought any cats lately or what exactly was the price of black toms now?

Not everyone made it in the north. One fall day, with a passenger, I landed at MacDougall's while southbound. Roy told us that earlier that day they had had a visit from a new pilot from Prince George. He said who it was and we both knew him, but didn't say anything. Then, Roy looked at me and said, "I didn't like him!" Thus, the word would go out on the moccasin telegraph that Roy MacDougall, the most respected man in the north, didn't like this particular individual. And the poor soul would never know the full, human warmth the north was capable of exhibiting. Actually, this particular person had a much worse fate. He did not survive a crash he had in his aircraft a year or two later.

These northern posts received mail once a month, nine times a year. Two months were allowed in the fall for freeze-up and one month in the spring for break-up. Air service was started in the 1930s and changed very little over the years. On the morning of the day the mail plane was due, the bench below the trading post would have about a dozen Native tents set up. Everyone in the family always came to the post on mail day, winter or summer. When the mail came they would cash their monthly government checks, stock up on food and supplies, along with a few treats for the kids, then the following day they would be gone, appearing again the next mail day.

Summer time, especially after high-water in July when most of the driftwood would clear from the rivers, was a very busy time for the river freighters. All the trading posts would be stocked with everything they expected they would need for the next year. Major customers for river freight were the bush airlines. They would have hundreds of forty-five-gallon drums of aviation gas stored at the posts for their use throughout the year.

One fall when the rivers were low I came to Finlay Forks. As soon as I landed Roy asked me if I had seen Art Van Somer on the river. When I told him I hadn't, he said Art was eight days overdue from Fort McLeod and asked if I would look for him on my return trip. I said I would, but that I wouldn't be going south until the next day. The next day when I landed at Finlay Forks, Roy said Art had come in a short time after I had left the day before. Art had a load of thirty drums of aviation gas, and on the many miles of shallow water and shifting sand bars on the Parsnip River, he said numerous places were too shallow to float the load. Art said he couldn't remember how many times he and his bowman had to unload most of the drums, float the lighter load through the shallows, then roll the barrels to the boat and reload! Each drum of gas weighed 400 pounds. Northern life wasn't always fun and adventure.

Dick Corless sometimes guided people, usually nonresidents, on a sort of adventure and fishing trip. One of his favorite places to take them was where the Wicked River joined the Peace. The little Wicked was crystal clear and in the mini-canyon near its mouth were pools twelve or more feet deep. Large grayling fish would lie on the bottom. Cast a small, black dry-fly on the surface and the fish would come to it right from the bottom. As a bonus, this was virtually in the shadow of beautiful Mount Selwyn.

Fifty air miles (at least twice that by water) north of Finlay Forks was the oldest and most historic post on the Finlay River—Fort Graham. In 1897-98 the members of the Royal Northwest Mounted Police who were attempting to cut a trail to the Yukon gold fields on the Klondike River wintered there. Early in the new century it had a Hudson's Bay store, police, church, quite a few residents and later a government wireless communication station. For two or three years after about 1912, the famous pioneer surveyor Frank Swannell used Fort Graham as his base. Trails fanned out in all directions from the post, especially to the west, making it a favorite base for prospectors and trappers. Graham was built on a bench just above the river on the east side. The bench kept steadily eroding into the river and the flood of 1948 washed away the bank from under many of the old buildings. That site was then abandoned and what was left of Fort Graham moved to the west side of the river.

When I knew Fort Graham, there was, on the west side of the Finlay, just one long log building with a partition near one end. Ben Corke lived in the smaller end and had his trading post and post office in the other part. One summer day I had supper with him, listened throughout the evening to stories, then rolled my sleeping bag out on the floor in the trading post for the night.

Ben said that in the 1930s there were placer miners on every bar on the Finlay River. He bought their gold using a balance with beans for counter-weights until the government made him get a proper scale. From then on he said he never made any money buying gold! He probably got most of the money paid for the gold back through purchases from his post, anyway.

Some Natives came from as far as 125 miles to Fort Graham for their mail. Again, every member of the family would come. The infants were carried, but from the age of about three years, four at the most, they had to walk! Here, too, their tents would appear like magic on the morning of the day the mail plane would arrive. Ben Corke claimed they had a sixth sense and knew if the plane would be delayed. Weather plays a major role in bush flying and it was not uncommon for the mail plane to be delayed for one or more days. Ben said on the morning the mail was due he would look at the clearing near the post. If the tents were there, he said the plane would come; if there were no tents, he just went about his regular business knowing the mail plane wouldn't arrive! He said he never knew them to be wrong over many years of observation.

If the Natives brought in wild fur, the pelts would be purchased before the plane arrived. Then when the mail came, Ben would sort it while his store was packed with people. The Natives would then take their government checks and turn them over to Ben in exchange for clothes, supplies, ammunition, tobacco, etc. The next day the mail would go south.

About seventy-five air miles above Graham was (is) Fort Ware. Most of the river en route was excellent for riverboats, but there was one serious obstacle—Deserters Canyon. This was a nasty, crooked gorge complete with huge standing waves and a "hole in the water," caused by a vicious whirlpool, as well as a jagged rock sticking up in the middle of the river. The river freighters often had to split up their load and relay it through the canyon. Over the years they hauled a tremendous amount of freight through the canyon, partly because the airlines maintained a major fuel cache at Fort Ware. That none of the freighters were drowned just proves what great rivermen they were.

The HBC started a post at Ware in 1927, built a new store about 1947 and then abandoned the place in 1953. Ben Corke ran it off-and-on from 1954 until 1963, the year before he died. I was at Fort Ware twice during the summer of 1955. The first time there wasn't a single soul present and the other time there was one Native family. Ben Corke was operating the post from the old HBC store, when I landed there one February day just after lunch. Ben sliced a huge steak from a fresh haunch of moose for me. I was thinking that a moose shot at that time of year wouldn't taste very good and I was afraid I wouldn't be able to eat it all and would be embarrassed. But it was delicious and I saved my integrity by eating the whole thing! At that time Ben actually alternated between Ware and Graham. Sometimes he would operate one post, other times the other one. This set the stage for a dramatic event.

During a very cold spell one January, Merv Hesse, flying for Pacific Western Airlines, had to make a trip to Ware. It wasn't a scheduled flight, Ware wasn't getting mail then, and I think the build-up to the flight went something like this. Milt Warren heard Merv say he had to go to Ware one of these days and Milt said, "Go tomorrow and I'll go with you."

So just after daylight they left Prince George on a clear, cold morning. About half way between Graham and Ware, Milt spotted a person sitting in the snow on the river ice, frantically waving at them. Merv landed the old Junkers airplane beside the hapless soul and they discovered it was Ben Corke. Ben had been at Fort Ware and, for some long-forgotten reason, decided he had to go to Fort Graham, so he set out on snowshoes! Now, a snowshoe trip of nearly 100 wilderness miles during a very cold spell in the dead of a northern winter and the short daylight hours of January is no mean feat for anyone. But Ben was over sixty and had lost a leg below his knee in World War One, thus he walked on a wooden leg. Part way into the trip the stump got sore. He carried on, but by the time the fellows landed beside him, it was so sore and swollen that he couldn't put any weight on it. It was unlikely that he would have survived one more night.

But fate decreed that the trip to Ware would be made that day.

Fate also ruled that Ben would be on the river ice where he could be seen and not in the bush, where the snowshoe trail was located for much of the way. And fate had the aircraft over the twisting river where Ben sat, virtually helpless, while Milt in the right-hand seat was able to observe the helpless man.

That tale is typical of the many dramas enacted in the hinterlands. The story of two trappers murdered on the ice of the Lower Finlay and the apprehension and hanging of the murderer is told in a book of B.C. police stories with game warden Alf Janke, then stationed in the area, playing a major role. But, alas, so many anecdotes will never again be told and no one will ever know of them because so many of those who could tell the stories are gone. How much history went with Dick Corless and Art Van Somer?

When the northern trappers and prospectors came out to so-called civilization, Prince George was the usual destination. And for some unknown reason, it was always the old Canada Hotel that became their home away from home. This place was not known as an up-scale, high quality establishment and it would never appear in a tourist brochure. However, it seemed to suit the trappers and prospectors just fine.

Milt Warren knew all the northerners and always seemed to know when any of the them were in town. He would tell me, then we would go to the Canada in the evening and assist the men from the north in wetting their whiskers in the foamy, which by the way, cost ten cents for a large glass full. What a shame we didn't have a tape recorder, which could have put so many stories into permanent history.

We always had a very enjoyable evening at these get-togethers. I remember one little incident that occurred the first time I met Lou Strandberg. He lived in town when he wasn't trapping, but I had never met him and was just introduced as a friend of Milt's. There was another trapper from the north at the table, so I just sat there listening, saying nothing. Wild mountain sheep inhabited only very few, widely scattered areas in the entire country I write about and very little was known of them, including just what mountains they lived on. The talk got around to wild game, when I leaned over to Lou and said, "There are sheep on XX creek." Lou Strandberg nearly choked on his beer, then he stared at me in utter disbelief. To add to his dismay, the name I called the creek was the local, northern name for it, not the name of it on the map. After a long, hard stare, he said, "And how did you know there are sheep on XX creek," using the same local name I had used. Thinking I was just another dude from town, he was completely bewildered. My answer, the one I've often used, was just, "Oh, I get around." Of course, that didn't satisfy him and later in the evening he again wondered aloud how I knew there were sheep on XX creek.

One fine summer evening Milt Warren phoned to tell me that a certain old trapper was in town, so we went to the Canada Hotel to see him. For reasons that you will later guess, I will not give his name or the area he came from. He was an outstanding, old veteran northerner of Norwegian descent, like so many of the old-time northerners were. He was of the breed of trappers who came out to any settlement only when they really had to. In his case he may not show up at Fort Graham, the nearest trading post, even once a year. I suppose if he hadn't shown up at Graham for more than two years, someone would say they had better check up on him!

Thus, it was quite an event for him to get to Prince George. And not only was he in that town, but he was on his way to Vancouver! He said he had a sister there whom he hadn't seen for nearly forty years. This fellow was also a prospector, as many of the trappers were. Since they were only interested in commercial minerals, I would always ask if they had come across any crystals of any kind. This old prospector drew me a map of an area where he said there were lots of crystals, clear quartz and other "colored ones."

During the evening Milt asked him if he had just left his cabin as it was. He said, "I left my rifle at Fort Graham." Out of the clear blue I said, "How about the other gun?" He looked at me, showed with his hands that "the other gun," which of course I didn't know existed, was a revolver. He then said he had greased it, put it in a pail with a lid and buried it near his cabin.

When, late in the evening we said our good-byes, it was the last time that any of us would ever again see him. Word came that he had died in Vancouver.

I know exactly where his cabin was. After all these years I think it would be a terrific memento of the north to have his pistol that has been buried near his cabin for all that time. And after the metal detector locates it, I may just spend some time looking for those crystals!

The saga of the area I write of even includes suspected buried treasure of commercial value. It has been calculated that Pete Toy, in the 1870s, mined $70,000 worth of gold from the bar named after him when gold was probably $16 an ounce. He never left the area or sold the gold, but was soon drowned in the Omineca River. His gold must have been buried somewhere nearby but now would be ensconced under two or three hundred feet of water.

The people of the north talked about the trader who made big money over the years, wouldn't put it in a bank because he never trusted banks, then died. These people were certain there was a buried cache of wealth from him. If this horde exists, it will certainly be above the water level!

In 1958, British Columbia's centennial, the committee in charge of provincial celebrations built a huge canoe to be paddled from Fort St. James to Fort Langley by a group of men to emulate Simon Fraser's early, historic deed. Dick Corless was chosen to be Simon Fraser. He asked me if I would be one of his paddlers. I said I couldn't make because of the time away from work, but he asked me a second time. I still didn't go, though often wished I would have just taken the time, but I considered it an honor to have been asked.

Eventually, the flood from the dam came and ended everything. Not only was the land gone and the people moved from the area I write of, but the time coincided with the ending of an entire way of life in the hinterlands. A great era was over; passed into history. So gently and so unobtrusively did it go, that mainstream life never blinked or even noticed! Even the historians have for the most part largely ignored this great segment of our past. And the vast majority of those great people of the north were men who never married or left heirs to perpetuate Grampa's stories.

Gone forever, gone with little trace that he ever existed, was the independent prospector with his dog, his single-shot .22 rifle, a large pack on his back and a maze of stories he would gladly share with you, if he liked you. Gone were the old-time trappers from their neat and cozy little log cabins that once adorned the banks of the beautiful rivers and sat silently and lonely among the evergreen trees beside so many, often unnamed, picturesque creeks. Departed are the hardy souls who sometimes only came out to a settlement once a year. Gone are those splendid people from the trading posts and from the bush who would help you in any way possible, if you needed help. The flooding ended everything so abruptly and so permanently. And those of us who were there will have to put it all into memory. From time to time we'll try to relate it to those souls unfortunate enough to have missed it. But in spite of our best effort, we will never be completely successful in our endeavor.

How do you describe the feeling when you look at the fancy knick-knacks in a veteran trapper's cabin, fashioned by an old Norwegian with just his ax, saw and jackknife, and know that not even a handful of people will ever see them? Or the feeling you get when you land at a trading post two days after the last mail plane of the winter and the first words you hear from the post operator are, "Thank goodness you came. Now I can get that letter sent that missed getting in the mail. You saved me two months on a message I really wanted sent." How do you relate the character of the old trapper that gives you the use of his cabin for several days, loans you his only row boat to get there and then won't take a cent for it! Or the northerner's unique way of giving directions. I asked the old trapper how would we find the spot seven miles up a strange lake, where a path would start, leading a half-mile into the bush to his cabin. He looked at me, then simply stated in his thick Norwegian accent, "You will have no trouble, I blazed a jack-pine tree." End of the directions! Incidentally, we did find the correct blazed pine tree on the first attempt. And half a mile down the path, beside a fast-flowing little creek with crystal clear water, was the finest, cleanest trapper's cabin one would ever see.

Marge and Roy MacDougall moved to Vancouver Island in 1960, right after they sold the post. I went to see them at the airport in Prince George while they were waiting to go on the airliner. It was not a happy occasion. I had never seen them so quiet, and I was completely stumped as to what to say. Actually, I think I felt about as bad as they did. A fabulous country and a great way of life was gone.

Chapter 2

Historical Fort McLeod

History buffs will know the first white settlement west of the Rocky Mountains in British Columbia was Fort McLeod, near the north end of McLeod Lake, about eighty-five miles north of present-day Prince George. In recent times, relatively few people realize the historical significance of the area that surrounded the Fort.

The Northwest Company established this most southerly post on the Arctic watershed west of the Rocky Mountains in 1805, and then it was absorbed into the historic Hudson's Bay Company in 1821, when that pioneer firm took over the Northwest Company. Trading posts operated continuously near the north end of McLeod Lake, right up to the one I knew in the 1950s, which was an independent, privately operated post. Fort McLeod was the most southerly of the four or five trading posts that started receiving airmail services in the 1930s. The mail service was once a month, nine times a year, the same as for the posts in the Rocky Mountain Trench.

In 1952 the gravel-surfaced Hart Highway (now Highway 97) was completed from Prince George to Dawson Creek, going past McLeod less than half a mile from the trading post. But for several years after, Fort McLeod carried on almost oblivious to the modern world going by so near. To go from the highway down the hill on the little, narrow, rutted one-way road to the end of the lake was a trip back in time. The old airmail contract was still in place, bringing the mail nine times a year, when it could have come weekly, or even daily, by bus.

During the decade of the 1950s I was flying throughout the general area and I "discovered" Fort McLeod early in that period. The heart of the settlement was a nice log building that housed the W-M Trading Post, operated by Justin McIntyre, a real old-timer of the area always referred to as "Mac." Mac told me that in 1911 he was part of a survey crew that was attempting to locate a suitable route for crossing the Rocky Mountains. He told me the route they chose and surveyed was nearly identical to the route the Hart Highway would follow through Pine Pass forty years later!

When the mail arrived at Mac's post the entire Native population from McLeod came across the bay at the end of the lake from their village and crowded into the post until the mail was sorted. In the summer they often sat on the floor of the veranda. I watched one very elderly, fine, well-known lady sitting on the floor in complete contentment, quietly smoking her large, curved stem pipe while people just walked around her. Trading post operators, of course, built a reputation, good or bad, over the years, and Mac was highly respected, very well liked and trusted by all who knew him, be it Natives or white people. Without question, the two trading post operators most highly respected and completely trusted were the MacDougalls of Finlay Forks and Justin McIntyre of Fort McLeod.

Mac had gold scales, enabling him to purchase gold from the placer operations of some of his clients. He also accepted their trapped fur for cash or trade on his store goods. His trading goods were typical of those found in any northern post; basic groceries, some goodies like cookies and chocolate bars, tobacco, a few shoes, boots and clothes, ammunition, maybe a rifle or two, as well as such diverse articles as files, water pails and traps.

The fascination of the place came from the unique characters who either hung out or stopped over there and from the customs of the north still practiced. The major customers of the post were the local Natives, but every trapper, trader, prospector or old-timer came to Mac's post whenever they were traveling to or from the north. Indeed, Mac and his post were actually part of the north, indelibly tied to every facet of northern life. Thus, his store became the southern terminal of the "moccasin telegraph." This was the great communication system of the hinterlands. In the part of the world we are talking about here, Finlay Forks was the heart of the moccasin telegraph system. All news funneled in and out of that post, thus the MacDougalls were aware of all happenings throughout the entire, huge area. Most news from the north also found its way to Justin McIntyre's Fort McLeod post.

Every northerner that came through told Mac all he had heard along the way, and then Mac would pass that on to the next traveler. Thus, everyone, though seemingly isolated, would soon learn such things as who was prospecting on the Akie (Ak-eye-ee), who had swamped his boat in Black Canyon or what fur buyer flew in, attempting to buy fur at a low price for cash. Or maybe they heard about which two trappers were in a bit of a squabble over blaming each other for attracting beaver to their own side of a stream and, thus, to their legal trapping area!

Just how thorough, how effective and how everyone was involved in the moccasin telegraph, whether they knew it or not, was one time demonstrated very clearly to me. Milt Warren, who knew virtually everyone in the north, and I were sitting in a cafe on the highway near McLeod Lake drinking coffee when a man whom Milt knew, but I had never seen before, sat down with us. Milt didn't bother to introduce me and he and the new man started talking. Mining and prospecting were big-time activities in that era and the rumor mill ran overtime spinning tales of great prospects almost found!

Soon the new man at our table leaned toward Milt and in low tones started telling a story he had heard about a potential mineral strike, supposedly of rich proportions. When he had finished his tale, Milt said, "It can't be very good or Bruce Lamb would be there!"

"I know," said the man, "he'd be there for sure, if it was any good."

Here was a man who had never seen me before, did not know that he was now sitting beside me, but immediately recognized my name and thought I would be one of the people looking at it, as it was normal for anyone interested in prospecting to check out a new find. All of this came courtesy of the great moccasin telegraph and, oh yes, I showed no reaction whatsoever, and the stranger never learned of the joke played on him! Milt loved a good joke and we enjoyed many of them.

Sooner or later a customer would come to McLeod Post and say, "Hey Mac, I get jawbone?" This was the true, time-honored way of asking for credit at any trading post in the hinterlands, since time immemorial. The question is asked but framed as a statement of fact. The word "jawbone," meant they wanted to get something now and pay for it later. Sometimes only the vital word, "jawbone," would be spoken. This was probably the closest point to the modern world that one could still hear the phrase used in its somber, meaningful purpose. Mac, like any other trader, would hesitate and then ask, "What do you want?" If it was an item, or items, of necessity, they would likely get it, with the promise to pay when the next mail brought the monthly check or be taken from the proceeds of the next fur sold.

Mac also had two neat and clean log cabins, equipped with stoves, bunks and mattresses, that people often slept in, but not in exchange for money. Only Mac's friends slept in the cabins and Mac didn't charge his friends! I always felt proud of the fact that I soon became a trusted friend of Mac and his northern pals, and I, too, slept in the cabins.

One winter afternoon while flying from the north I was running out of daylight so I landed on McLeod Lake. Mac's first words were, "Oh dear, the cabins are both occupied, but I think there's room in the big one." The "big one" had a second bunk behind a skimpy partition. An old friend of Mac's, a geologist from Alaska, and his wife were spending the night in the cabin, but it was fine with them if I, too, stayed there. I had a very enjoyable evening with the jovial couple, and then rolled out my sleeping bag on the extra bunk that exhibited some semblance of privacy.

Friends of Mac would also, on occasion, be invited to his living quarters in the back room for tea. This was quite a ritual. Mac would stoke-up the wood range, fill a pot with water, put a lid on it, then sit and visit while it heated. The pot was the type with a solid handle protruding from the side, near the top. When it boiled, he would carefully measure some tea in his hand, place it in the boiling water, and then soon it would be ready to drink.

One time while enjoying tea and a visit, I asked Mac if anyone knew the exact location of the original post of the Northwest Company, built in 1805. He answered, "We think we do. When I came here shortly after 1900, I asked that question, and the hand-me-down word of mouth information given by both the Indians and white people agreed on the same spot." With that, Mac slowly rose from his chair and I followed him through the store to the picturesque veranda on the front of the large, log-walled trading post. He then pointed the direction, gave the distance and explained the location, just as he had been told a half century before. Thus, at this point in history, I may very well be the last person with direct, hand-me-down information on the location of the original post, the first white settlement in B.C. west of the Rocky Mountains!

I was amused several years ago. A couple, a man and wife well known for their many articles published in magazines, visited the area. Their custom was to travel through an area once, then write lengthy articles about the country's history. They traveled to the north end of McLeod Lake by canoe from Summit Lake. They had a long article printed in a popular British Columbia outdoor magazine. In their story they stated it was too bad someone didn't restore the original Fort McLeod site, while you could still see where it was! They said even the circle of rocks that once ringed the flagpole was still there. What they had seen belonged to the third post built, not the first one! So much for history as printed in glossy magazines, written by professional writers whose research was cursory at best.

Regular northern travelers included the commercial river freighters Dick Corless and Art Van Somer, who, as stated in a previous chapter, loaded all their freight at Fort McLeod after the highway came by. When a riverboat crew returned, Mac would hear all the news from the north, such as what big mining company had a geologist flown into what area for an inspection of a prospector's property.

A prospector who from time to time would stop at McLeod was a small, slight, wizened-looking man who must have been well into his sixties, but he always carried a monstrous-sized pack on his back. He would come, stay in one of the cabins for a few days, stock up on supplies from Mac, and then just disappear. Maybe in a month, or maybe three, he would stop in again. But he seldom told anyone where he had been, where he was going or when he would be back. He wouldn't even tell Mac, a trusted friend. The best Mac could tell us was, "I think he has been in such-and-such valley or river area," but Mac was just making an educated guess. The prospector was known simply as "Old Holmes."

One time a well-known prospector and I planned to stake a placer lease for each of us. Early on a muggy July day, when the flies and mosquitoes would be at their biting best, we put our equipment for the day in the prospector's riverboat. Just before we pushed-off, Old Holmes came with his ax and a small pack, then without a word, climbed into the boat with us! When we beached the boat we still had four bush-miles to walk. We worked hard all day, blazing long claim boundaries through wet, mosquito- and fly-infested bush, then walked the four miles back and took the boat to the post. Holmes just passed off our thanks with a that-was-nothing shrug, and at the end of the day I knew nothing more about Old Holmes than I had in the morning!

Another veteran prospector, Bill McFee, living then at McLeod, told me of some of his earlier life, all of which was spent in the northern wilderness. One summer when he was teamed with the legendary prospector Shorty Weber, they were prospecting 140 miles west of Fort Graham. They were running out of grub, but Shorty stayed on, saying they were close to a big find. Finally, one morning their last bit of food, their flour mix, was baked into one bannock in the frying pan! It was time to head out on the 140-mile trail to Fort Graham—without a find.

The first day of travel, Shorty shot a large ground squirrel. He skinned and dressed it, then stuck it on a stick over the fire. But while it was still nearly raw, he ate it. The young prospector said he was so sickened by the sight of blood running through Shorty's whiskers and down his chin, that he walked all the way to Fort Graham on just his half of the one bannock! Shorty continued to eat a nearly raw ground squirrel every day of the journey, about four or five days.

Bill McFee was disappointed in himself and the way he had spent his young life. He said all his prime years had been spent in the mountains and bush of the north and he had completely missed out on a normal life. One day I sat in his cabin, at his invitation to come and have coffee with him, and listened as the bachelor poured out his deepest feelings to me. There was a definite feeling of sadness in me when I finally left him in his cabin.

There were a lot of extremely competent bushmen in the country at that time. Most were completely at home in the bush and it was extremely rare for one of them to get into serious trouble in the wilderness, though they often spent most of the time by themselves. Shorty Weber's name always stood out as being among the best in the bush at the art of surviving. I have talked to other people who had traveled with Shorty in the wilderness. They told me he never carried a sleeping bag, blankets or a tent. He took with him a quite heavy, long coat. At night he would sit on some tree boughs while leaning back against a tree and sleep! If it was cold he would have a fire in front of him, which he would stoke up, from time to time, opening the coat to catch the heat. If it was raining or snowing, the tree he leaned against would be an evergreen, with thick, long branches to turn away moisture. Shorty Weber would be dry in the morning, but he never lied down to sleep when he was in the bush!

There was an unofficial connection to the old Fort McLeod settlement on the highway half a mile away. There was a restaurant run by Mrs. Landon, who knew all of Mac's friends and northerners. This was where they all ate whenever they bought a meal. In fact, her establishment could be termed a branch line of the moccasin telegraph, because she, too, shared all the northern news. When I would come in, especially if I hadn't been around for a while, she would immediately come to my table. In her rapid style of talking she would tell me all the latest news, sometimes to the detriment of someone waiting to be served! I thoroughly enjoyed it, because she would often have a feminine viewpoint on things, making it more interesting than when told by a male prospector or trapper.

One evening I went to her restaurant with two foresters I was flying to worksites in the area while we stayed at a nearby lodge. Mrs. Landon was catching me up on all the news, when she came to a name she couldn't remember. She looked at me and said, "You know who I mean." I couldn't think of who she could be talking about, so I said, "No, I don't know who that would be." One of the foresters almost gagged, when he burst out laughing at her reply. She said to me, "You do so know who it is, you know him as well as I do!"

What a shame that people would come in from the highway, have a meal and go without ever knowing how close they had been to a completely different world had they only driven down the little trail to the old trading post. Imagine, if you will, how a modern-day reporter would like to go back in time and sit with a group of old-timers on the veranda of Justin McIntyre's trading post! But, alas, it can never be. The fabulous world we knew that existed on the north end of McLeod Lake is long gone.

The end of the era started with the post office moving from Mac's store to a new building on the highway; it changed the name from Fort McLeod to McLeod Lake and got regular mail service. Next, Justin McIntyre died. All northern river travel ceased when the Peace River Dam flooded all the beautiful land to the north, including the drowning of two historical trading posts. The old prospectors simply faded away and not only from the old fort. The day of the independent, pick-and-shovel, backpacking prospector was over and old Fort McLeod was no more. Never again would the long, wooden river boats be docked at the pier while those hardy northern travelers, the veteran river freighters, loaded the boats with heavy loads, destined for a far-off trading post or a lonely trapper's cabin beside a river.

A few years ago my wife, Florence, and I stopped at McLeod with our truck and travel trailer, on a trip home from Alaska. Florence had seen it as it once was, because many years previous I had taken her there. We had tea with Mac, then she purchased a pair of Indian-made moccasins from him.

It was a quiet, deserted, desolate-looking sight that confronted us. The old log building that was once the W-M Trading Post was still standing, but a car with a license plate from another province was parked in the yard. The once-tidy cabins were still there but in various forms of disrepair. Even some of the old dock was still visible, pushed partly on shore at a twisted angle. As I walked around, taking in the forlorn scene, it was very easy to slide back in time.

I could stare at the big log building and see Mac put down his cup of tea, rise slowly from his chair and go out to serve a customer. From a trim log cabin I could see Old Holmes emerge, then start across the yard, walking with an exaggerated forward lean to counter the weight of an oversized pack. In my trip back in time I could see a silver-colored floatplane coming in low over the river mouth, flaps down for a landing near the dock. In the passenger front seat is a burly prospector. In the rear is piled his camping and prospecting equipment and lying on top of that is a monstrously big dog, contentedly looking out the aircraft's windows. The pilot at the controls is a young Bruce Lamb.

With mixed emotions we got in our vehicle and started for home.

CHAPTER 3

Two Brothers Lake

Y ou won't find it on a map, not by that name anyway, but in the 1930s this three-mile-long lake, hidden deep in the wilderness in a very remote, beautiful area of northern British Columbia, was a hub of activity. A rich placer gold deposit had been discovered on McClair Creek, a far-off tributary of the Finlay River, about eight miles west of the lake. This has often been referred to as the last major placer gold strike discovered in British Columbia.

Grant McConache, a famous second-generation Canadian bush pilot, was deeply involved in the flying associated with the gold mining. This is well documented in the book about his exploits, *Bush Pilot with a Briefcase*, by Ronald A. Keith. However, from talking with various people, some of whom worked at the placer mine, I was well aware of this operation long before I read the above-mentioned book.

I have referred to McConache as a second-generation pilot because he started flying in the 1930s. The pilots, mostly World War One veterans, who pioneered bush flying starting in the mid-1920s are known as first-generation bush pilots. However, Grant McConache went on to fame and his name would one day become a household word.

He became known for starting, and operating, Yukon Southern Air Transport Ltd., which ran scheduled flights from Vancouver to Whitehorse, Yukon, and from Edmonton to Whitehorse. These flights were run with modern, for the day, twin-engine aircraft with retractable landing gear and instrument flight capability. This all started prior to World War Two. Then, his fame spread rapidly when he became the first, and very popular, president of Canadian Pacific Airlines, Canada's second largest airline. After the war he was responsible for that company's world-wide expansion, including becoming the first Canadian airline to fly scheduled passenger service to Australia and parts of Asia.

But in the mid-1930s, Grant McConache was providing transportation for the placer gold mining operation on McClair Creek. He had two extra pilots and three old Fokker Universal aircraft, flying on skis and floats from Takla Landing on the lake of that name. Takla Landing was provided with summer time barge and boat service from the end of the road at Fort St. James, by way of Stuart Lake, Tachie River, Trembleur Lake, Middle River and then up Takla Lake to the Hudson's Bay post. From Takla Landing, everything was flown to Two Brothers Lake, about eight miles from the gold mine. Because the lake was so far from the mining operation, they flew in a Caterpillar 30, gas track-type tractor, to haul the freight from the lake to the mine. Since the airplanes could haul a maximum of little more than 1,000 pounds, the tractor had to be taken apart, flown in piecemeal and then reassembled at far-away Two Brothers Lake. Using the same procedure, a sawmill was flown in to cut lumber for the buildings. A large cookhouse, office and several little bunkhouses were built for a camp.

I have gone into this in some detail because of the important, maybe vital, part this would play in an incident I was involved in about twenty years later. When the mining operation was in its preliminary stage in the summer of 1933, four men were stranded at the lake due to an aircraft breakdown on the way in to get them. After more than a month delay, the men were picked up in a late state of starvation, just in time to prevent a major tragedy. Was this an omen of things to come?

Advance to the summer of 1955. The lake was still known to the prospectors and old-timers as Two Brothers, but its official name was shown on maps as Toodoggone, pronounced tooda-gone. A big-game outfitter obtained guiding rights over a huge area centered on Toodoggone Lake. Thus, he laid claim to the old buildings that once were home to the gold miners of McClair Creek.

The outfitter purchased seventeen horses in the Vanderhoof area, sixty-five miles west of Prince George. He hired guides, horse wranglers and an excellent young cook, about six people in all, who would take the horses overland to McClair Creek. For the first 160 miles they could use the backwoods road to Germansen Landing. But they still had a long way to go, probably as far as 200 miles, without trail by the route they would take. And that included swamps, dangerous rivers, mountains and thick bush.

Arrangements were made for me to fly to Toodoggone Lake and bring out the outfitter on July 28, 1955. The owner-outfitter had earlier been flown into the lake, along with a couple of helpers, to work on the camp. If the horse outfit had not yet arrived, the outfitter and I would look for them with the aircraft. However, when I arrived at the lake a guide met me, with an extra saddle horse for me to ride to the buildings about seven miles away. The men and horses had arrived at McClair Creek just a day prior to my arrival, having conquered the wilderness in fine condition and were in high spirits and a happy mood.

I tied the aircraft up for the night on Toodoggone Lake and climbed aboard the extra saddle horse for the trip to the old mine buildings. On the most westerly portion of the lake, at the end of a little bay, was a very interesting sight. The Caterpillar tractor that had been flown to the wilderness lake in pieces in bush planes, stood there, appearing in perfect condition! It was still hooked onto a "sloop." This is a device made of two logs for skids, with a platform on it, used for hauling the freight from the lake to the mining operation. It looked like it had been there for only a week instead of about twenty years! There was also a log cabin at the lake, larger than most bush cabins, that had been built and used in conjunction with the gold mining operation.

Coming with the horses were three guides, one or two horse wranglers and the cook, who brought a guitar with him and while on the trail composed a song with the chorus, "On the way up to the Cassiar, I rode a bay horse and I strummed a guitar." The lyrics described many of their hardships and experiences on the way and were really very well written and sounded great when sung by him as he picked his guitar. That evening spent at the old gold mine camp was one of those enjoyable times so often seen in the backwoods years ago. The men were in a happy mood, proud of their achievement of taking seventeen saddle and pack horses on a six-week epic trip through the northern wilderness and arriving at a dot on the map in perfect condition, without so much as a scratch on any man or beast. The young cook had just made a fresh batch of pastry, which we washed down with gallons of coffee as we joked, told stories and listened to the cook play his guitar and sing.

The outfitter went back to Prince George with me the next day, as planned. An airline that was doing bush flying was used in the fall to take hunters in and out and to supply the hunting camp. The outfitter went back with the first load of hunters. In mid-October they took out the last of the crew from the camp, intending to come back the next day and get a load of camp gear, consisting largely of the possessions belonging to the guides. But the day the aircraft was to go back, poor weather conditions prevented flying. The low-cloud, stormy condition was followed by a cold spell. When the aircraft finally returned to Toodoggone the lake was frozen over, preventing a landing with the float-equipped machine. Thus, all the belongings had to be left there, with the intention to pick them up later with a ski-equipped aircraft.

The outfitter had left his horses wintering in a valley. The winter started out with a lot of snow and the outfitter became worried about them, so he contacted me and made arrangements for me to fly to Toodoggone Lake and check on them. Since wolves could be a major problem, Milt Warren, who was the B.C. Game Department's official predator control officer, would go with me. A forty-five-gallon drum of aviation gas had been left at the lake. Our plan was to go to the lake, stay overnight in the cabin, then with the extra gas we would do our reconnaissance flights the next day and return home on the third day.

When a story or article depicts bush flying, it invariably shows a beautiful summer day with just a few light cumulus clouds in an otherwise clear sky. A float-equipped aircraft is usually shown tied to a dock on a pristine lake with just enough wind to lightly ripple the water. Well, those conditions can, and do, exist making life a joy for the pilot. What is never shown is a plane on a river, with the pilot attempting to get it on shore without damaging a float on rocks or hitting a tree with a wing tip.

However, it is the wintertime that really separates bush flying from any other. In the summer, glassy water on a lake is considered one of the hazards of landing a float plane, because the pilot can not see the water surface to judge his height above it. Many accidents have occurred because the pilot did not execute the proper glassy water procedure for a safe landing. In the winter this condition often exists in spades. This is because on a dull, heavy, overcast day in a land solidly covered in unbroken white snow often the pilot can't see anything! The sky at the horizon blends fully in with the snow-covered surface. In short, you can't tell up from down. It is extremely difficult to not only judge height, but to know if the aircraft is level or on its side, maybe going into a dive. In aviation jargon this condition is known as a "white-out" and has been the cause of many, many serious accidents. In the short days of winter some variation of this condition, such as flying while snow is falling or in a dull overcast condition over a frozen lake, is all too common in northern flying. It is impossible to see the surface of the snow-covered lake and landing on it is more difficult and much more hazardous than landing on glassy water in the summer on floats.

Grant McConache had made his first flight into Two Brothers (Toodoggone) Lake in the winter. His biographer waxes eloquently on the navigational and super flying skills involved in getting to such a far-away destination hidden deep in the wilderness of mountainous northern British Columbia. He tells how one snow-covered valley looks just like another and how the winter winds blowing through the high mountains buffeted his light aircraft around. No one familiar with the situation could find much fault with the author's descriptions.

On December 2, 1955, Milt Warren and I took off from Prince George headed for Toodoggone Lake. And, really, conditions were no different for us than they had been for Grant McConache some twenty years previous! No new roads had been built in the north. The vast network of logging roads that now blankets so much of the northern hinterlands had not even been thought of at that time. Grant had no radio; we had a short range radio that lost all contact with the world after less than thirty minutes of flying in a northerly direction from Prince George. The only navigational device either of us had was a crude, magnetic compass. Grant McConache had one large advantage over us. He made his first trip at the end of February when the winter days are getting considerably longer and the weather is usually much brighter with fewer snowstorms. December, when we went, is the worst month of the year for flying in the north. Few hours of daylight, long periods of semilight morning and afternoon, with a lot of dull, snowy days making white-outs a common occurrence.

Fifty minutes north of Prince George, long out of radio contact, we would see the last of any road, as the highway to Dawson Creek angled off to the right. Forty minutes later we would see smoke rising from the chimneys of the buildings at Finlay Forks. Another thirty-five minutes, two hours five minutes from take-off, we would see a thin plume of smoke rising from the chimney of the one log building that was Fort Graham. This would be the last indication of human habitation we would see on the Toodoggone trip.

The weather was not good. Heavy overcast, fairly low clouds accompanied by snow showers necessitated us keeping to the lower passes through the mountains. Thus, north of Fort Graham we would go up the Ingenika, then the Pelly River to Bower Creek, then over the pass to the big bend of the Upper Finlay, follow that river to Toodoggone Creek, then up that creek to the lake. An hour and forty minutes from Fort Graham we had Toodoggone Lake in sight. After circling the lake to try to get a reading on the condition of the ice and snow, we landed.

Winter snow and ice conditions on a lake can be many things. The snow can be windblown into hard drifts, just waiting to rip the undercarriage off of an aircraft if visibility is poor and the pilot can't see that it has drifted. Or, and this is very common in British Columbia, there could be water under the snow. Or, worst of all conditions, the ice may not be thick or strong enough to hold the weight of the aircraft. Water under the snow comes about as follows. The lake freezes over, then a lot of snow falls, the weight of which pushes the ice down, allowing water to flood over the ice. If the snow is not windblown, it will insulate the water and keep it from freezing.

Water under the snow can easily get an aircraft stuck in the slush, unable to move, with the danger of it freezing in, if the weather is cold. One precaution taken is to watch the skis after they have settled onto the snow in landing. If water appears the pilot quickly applies power and takes off again. Milt was watching the ski on his side as we landed on Toodoggone. He kept repeating, "no water," so I let the machine slow down.

I have always had a sixth sense, a sort of a premonition of things to come, especially active in my younger years. As we landed on the lake, the aircraft was sliding onto an area of windblown snow, a nearly certain indication of good ice in a cold country. I then did something I never ordinarily did, I let the aircraft come to a stop instead of taxiing into shore by the cabin. Milt asked me what I was doing, and I said I was going to check the ice. So I took the ax and chopped into it to see how thick it was. I chopped into the ice a distance of twelve inches, more than twice what was required, so we taxied to the cabin. A hole chopped near the cabin later, to get water for our use, went through eighteen inches of solid, blue ice.

Another little problem associated with winter flying is that the skis will freeze solidly to the snow overnight. To prevent this we got some small poles to park the airplane on for the night. Oh yes, there's something else. In the cold weather of the north, the engine will not start the next day without another precaution. We had to drain the oil into a pail to take into the cabin with us. The next morning we would heat it on the stove, put it back in the engine, then get it started before things cooled down.

The early bush flying crews got tired of doing this every morning, so during the late 1930s they invented a dilution system whereby gas from the gas tank was pumped into the oil with an electric pump before shut-down at night. This thinned the oil sufficiently to allow starting in anything except the severest of cold weather. The gas would evaporate from the oil the next morning, when the engine was warmed up prior to take off. Unfortunately, our aircraft did not have this dilution system on it.

When I took my commercial pilot license training in Vancouver early in 1953, Canadian Pacific Airlines personnel gave the ground school training for the two flying schools that were giving commercial pilot training. This airline that Grant McConache was president of was an amalgamation of the early bush-type airlines, employing most of the old-time veterans. The engineer who lectured us on aircraft engines, was the very one credited with developing the oil dilution system to which I refer! His name was Tommy Siers—arguably the most famous of the early engineers and a member of the aviation hall of fame. He received the McKee Trophy for 1940 for the development of this device that so facilitated cold weather starting. (The McKee Trophy was Canada's highest award in aviation, awarded annually to the person or, rarely, organization deemed to have made the greatest contribution to aviation for the year.) Tommy Siers enjoyed talking about his dilution system, and other aspects of early flying, to the three or four of us taking commercial ground school training with them.

The door was open on the cabin at Two Brothers Lake. A large footprint, with claw marks well out in front of the toes, in the soil of the dirt floor in the cabin gave mute and irrefutable evidence that a big grizzly had been in the cabin after the guides had been flown out in October. The bear had eaten any food that was left, including chewing up the coffee pot! His teeth badly dented the coffee percolator but didn't quite punch holes in it, so we still used the pot. Strangely, we had forgotten to take salt with us, but would you believe Milt found a lump of hardened salt on the dirt floor that the bear had left, I guess after he had licked as much of it as he wanted. Or, most likely, he picked up the salt thinking it was food, then spit it out when he got the briny taste. Regardless, it still tasted just fine!

The cabin had only a gunny sack over the window opening, but it had a large barrel-type heating stove that took long pieces of wood. The stove was sufficient for the fairly large cabin, but it took a ferocious amount of wood to keep it going. It didn't take long after a hearty fire was started for the pleasant heat given off by the big stove to create that distinctive, exhilarating sense of feeling and smell only experienced when a wood-fired heater is warming a log cabin in cold weather. The sensation is readily identified by anyone familiar with cabins, fires and cold temperatures, but is almost impossible to describe to those who have never experienced it. We soon had a good, hot meal eaten by the light from candles we had brought with us and early in the evening we rolled into our warm, down sleeping bags.

The drum of gas we needed and the goods belonging to the guides had been left across a bay of the lake, about a half-mile from the cabin. We intended to taxi the aircraft over there on the frozen lake. The next morning, by the light from a candle, we had our breakfast eaten and ready to go well before any light appeared in the eastern sky. By the time a sufficient amount of illumination appeared in the sky to turn black globs on the shore line into snow-covered green balsam trees, we had the aircraft engine running.

In spite of our effort to keep the skis from freezing down, the aircraft was stuck and wouldn't move under its own power. If there ever was a standard method of doing something, this is it for freeing an aircraft when the skis are stuck. With considerable power from the engine, pushing the control column forward will raise the tail off the ground. This I did, and when the tail was about knee high above the snow, I pulled the control back, to give the tail a bump when it hit the hard snow. The little jolt will usually free the stuck front skis. This maneuver has been acted out thousands of times in the frozen north without incident. However, this particular time, on the edge of lonely Toodoggone Lake, when I pulled the control column back, the tail of the aircraft sank right down into the snow! Milt and I looked at each other as I shut the engine down. We both knew something had gone very wrong.

The flat, steel spring that holds the tail ski assembly to the aircraft had broken cleanly. Many times I had jolted the tail down harder than this time to loosen frozen skis without any damage. And every aircraft that flies in the cold north has been subjected to the same treatment. Unfortunately, this time the very cold weather must have awakened the little gremlins who then ordered the steel spring to break!

With the emergency tools we always carried, we took the tail ski assembly off, including the broken spring. The thought that Tommy Siers and his old-time engineer buddies must have often been confronted with situations like ours entered my mind and I wondered what they would do. We talked things over, took stock of the situation and figured out a plan. By a streak of luck there was an approximately correct size steel bolt in our supplies; this would play a vital part in the plan to return the aircraft to flying condition. We didn't think we could bolt the fairly heavy ski itself back on because of the angled spring that had broken off. But, there, leaning against the cabin, was a small shovel. The spade would do for a ski, if only we had a hole through it and the piece of broken spring, we could bolt things back together. Since I was quite experienced in various forms of shooting, including some off-beat experiments, I said we could shoot a hole through the broken steel spring with my rifle!

We put the steel spring on the wood stove to warm it, so it wouldn't shatter, and then leaned it against a stump. The bullet made a perfect hole through the hard, steel spring! Next, we sawed the handle off the spade, close to the metal. One more shot and the metal spade handle also had a hole through it. The one bolt would hold the weight but wouldn't stop the shovel from pivoting. However, snowshoes are made with babiche—a tough rawhide lacing that forms the webbing. Milt, like all experienced northerners, always carried spare babiche with him in case he had to repair his snowshoes. So, with his strong babiche, Milt solidly secured the shovel handle to the repaired spring.

In December in the north, the days are very short. By the time we had everything back together it was too late to fly. We had to put the engine and wing covers back on the aircraft and prepare for the night. We had to work hard and fast during the rest of the daylight in order to get enough wood cut and hauled in to keep the big stove going throughout the long evening and for breakfast the next morning.

By the time daylight broke the following morning we had the engine running and ready to go. This time, of course, I wouldn't dare bounce the tail to get us moving, so Milt stayed out and while I revved the engine, he rocked the wings to break the skis loose.

When the aircraft started to slide I slowed the engine for Milt to get in. However, he put his feet on the hub of the ski, wrapped his arms around the wing strut, then leaned back away from the blast from the propeller and motioned for me to keep going. So we headed out across the bay toward the barrel of gas on the far shore, with Milt on the outside, standing on the ski hub. Half way over the bay the aircraft suddenly started to veer to the right. Full left rudder failed to straighten it, but I thought that would be because the shovel used for a tail ski wasn't steerable. Then...CRUNCH! The right side of the aircraft, the side Milt was riding outside on, went through the ice!

The sudden roll to the right as the ski went through the ice gave me the impression the wing was going to go through also, then the whole machine would slide into the lake. By pure instinct I had the door open and I was out the left side. But instinct played a much deeper role. Our sleeping bags were in the aircraft, in case of emergency, on our planned day flight. It was so instilled in me that a large, warm sleeping bag was of such vital importance in winter survival, that when I hit the ice, my sleeping bag was with me! Without thinking, or even knowing how I did it, I had reached in the back and pulled my sleeping bag out on the ice. It was just pure luck that it was my sleeping bag and not Milt's. The point was, I had a sleeping bag and I didn't have time to get the other one.

As it turned out the right wing tip hit solid ice, holding up the aircraft but sharply bending the wing. Milt had jumped from the ski as it went through and I don't think he even got his feet wet. When I hit the ice Milt hollered at me, "Don't move!" This was the first I had heard from him, and I was very relieved to find that he was clear and hadn't gone in the lake. Milt was a superb bushman, one of the rare group of people who knew all the tricks and nothing ever upset his composure or good judgment—a true survivor. His type is not to be confused with the modern "outdoorsman," who goes hunting for a week in the fall, taking everything with them, sometimes including the kitchen sink, then think they are good bushmen.

Milt was lying flat on the ice and he told me not to move until I had checked the ice. The engine was still running. It had snowed about an inch and a half the night before and the turning propeller was cutting this thin layer of snow! Had the machine settled another two inches, the propeller would have hit ice and likely wrecked the engine.

After shutting down the engine, I took the ax from the plane to test the ice. It was good enough around me to support my weight, so I tossed the ax under the plane to Milt and soon we were able to get together and take stock of the situation.

On falling through the ice, the right front ski had collapsed and bent in the middle at a right-angle. The wing tip had hit the ice so hard that it also was bent quite sharply, including the aileron. Later, in a report written in the *Prince George Citizen*, December 15, 1955, they had the tail ski being broken when we went through the ice. But newspapers often get things mixed up, and the tail ski assembly was broken exactly as told in this narrative. Regardless, we were now thoroughly stranded at Toodoggone Lake!

No blame was placed on anyone. I couldn't see anything different looking about the area with thin ice, and Milt, riding on the outside, couldn't either. However, if it hadn't been for the light snowfall of the night before, we may have spotted something. Later, when we were able to freely walk around the weak area, I put a weight on our emergency fish line to check the depth of the water. The line was forty feet long, but the weight would not touch the bottom! A warm spring under the bed of the lake was the cause of the thick ice on the lake being so dangerously thin at this spot.

We discovered there was virtually no ice around the front of the aircraft. Somehow, sometime, the aircraft would have to be retrieved from the lake, and in order to do a successful retrieval a solid base would be required. Therefore, we decided to cut poles, drag them to the airplane, lay them side by side and throw water over them to form an ice bridge. We went to the nearest shore with suitable trees, cut some poles, skidded them to the plane and then carefully pushed them in place. After flooding the poles with water, we snowshoed to where the guides had left their equipment.

When the guides left, they had placed all their articles on the ground and covered everything with a huge tarp. However, we discovered that after they had gone, a grizzly bear had been at work. No doubt it was the same bear who later pushed open the door on our cabin and made himself at home in there. He had ripped off the tarp, tearing many holes in it and then went thoroughly and completely through everything.

Without our snowshoes on, the snow was more than knee-deep. We would kick through the snow at a lump showing, then see what it was. We would see a canvas kit bag that had been filled with personal belongings. But the bear had ripped it apart and scattered the contents. We would find such things as pictures, diaries, shaving equipment and letters from home. We saw where he had eaten a tube of toothpaste and then spit out the chewed up tube! Almost everything had teeth marks in it. There were prescription glasses in the old-fashioned, cloth-lined, metal case. The grizzly had bit the case, shattering a lens. Down sleeping bags were ripped apart, as were clothes such as jackets and pants. There was a Winchester lever-action rifle, in two pieces! It was broken at the small part of the stock.

All in all, it was an awful mess. The bear had scattered the good, and sometimes even precious, articles over an area nearly as large as the size of an ordinary house. Because of the deep snow we obviously didn't begin to see all the items that had once been left under the heavy, large tarp for protection. One good thing about it was there were some articles we could use in our work ahead. One thing left at the lake, still intact, was a single-shot shotgun, in the small .410 gauge. We also found four shells for it, and one afternoon with the first shot fired I got three ptarmigan to augment our food supply.

Back at the cabin we took stock of the situation. On a flight such as we had made, which is planned to extend into days, it is impossible to file a formal flight plan with the Department of Transport due to too many uncertainties. Therefore, all you can do under such circumstances is to leave the details of the trip, including, of course, when you expect to return, with a responsible person. In this case it was a brother, but as you will see later, he wasn't listening too well!

We were in about the remotest spot in British Columbia. Take a 1955 map of B.C., which will not include the present Stewart-Cassiar Highway, and pick out an area as far from any road or human habitation that you can find. The spot you pick on the map will likely be very close to Toodoggone Lake! Under the best of conditions I had said we would be back in three days, but at home they were not to get upset if we didn't get back until the fourth day. It was now well into the third day and our aircraft was through the ice in a lake and damaged, precluding any chance of getting home on schedule, so a ski-equipped airplane would likely pick us up on the fifth day.

Cutting wood for the big stove was a major daily chore. We had a Swede saw, now a collector's item, but smaller versions of it are still made called, by the rather wimpish name, a bow saw. We would have to find a dry tree, cut it down, cut it into stove-length pieces and carry it into the cabin. Dead trees were quite scarce, requiring that we go to ever-increasing distances from the cabin for the wood. We could use some green wood, mixed with the dry, and green trees were plentiful, but a goodly amount of dry wood was still required.

The rather large cabin took much more wood to heat than would a smaller cabin. This is the reason the very practical trappers and prospectors built small cabins. The small, well-built cabins were even of low height, just tall enough to accommodate the old-timer who was building it. They were very efficient, requiring only a small stove and a minimum amount of wood to heat them. The height of our cabin was proof it had been built by the men flown in from the south to work at the placer mine in the 1930s and not by seasoned bushmen!

The next morning we got more poles in place around the aircraft and more water on them to freeze, then we marked a landing strip with evergreen trees to facilitate the landing of a ski plane in poor visibility. Next, we used tree bows to make a message in the snow. This was in case a plane not equipped with skis came over. Our message said, "OK - PLANE US" (unserviceable).

After that we would spend the mornings securing a solid, frozen base around the airplane, while much of the afternoon was spent cutting wood. We had survival food, but not as much as we would have liked and a variation in diet would certainly be welcomed. We knew the outfitter had left food in a root cellar at his camp, so about day four we decided to snowshoe to the camp and replenish our food supply. Before we left we wrote a note to leave in the cabin, explaining where we had gone, for the search plane we were so sure would arrive, maybe while we were away.

By trail it was about seven miles to the outfitter's camp and the snow was quite deep and soft, making it tough going to break trail with our snowshoes. It was a cold, rather miserable day, with a north wind gathering snow from the trees and sifting it through the bush coating us with snow and frost.

After we arrived at the camp, made a fire and cooked a good meal, we were just too comfortable to even consider venturing out into the cold north wind! So we stayed at the old camp, built by the placer miners in the 1930s and more recently used by the big game outfitter, then snowshoed "home" the next day, listening in vain for the sound of the search plane we were so sure would soon be overhead. In Milt's Trapper Nelson packboard and bag that was always on his back, we placed a side of bacon, some flour and butter, along with other goodies such as dried eggs and strawberry jam. The larder the outfitter had left was better stocked with food than we had thought it would be! It seemed like a lot of food we took, but two young men working hard in that cold weather developed a magnum-sized appetite.

Under the eave of the cabin at the lake was very little snow. One of us noticed a chain, which we tried to pull out, then discovered it was a chain block, sometimes called "chainfalls." The block consists of a continuous chain in a loop configuration and two geared sprockets with hooks. In use, the one hook is fastened securely to something solid, while the other hook is connected to the load to be lifted. Pulling on the chain to rotate it will, because of the difference in size of the two sprockets and the gearing, slowly lift the load. The chain block lying in front of us would lift at least a ton and a half easily enough to retrieve our aircraft from the lake! This device was undoubtedly flown in by Grant McConache's firm to be used for reassembling the Caterpillar tractor. Also, without doubt, it had lain unused under the eave of the cabin ever since. Remember earlier in this narrative when I said the gold mining operation of the 1930s played a major role in our incident? The cabin, the chain block, what would we have done without them?

Our frozen ice bridge made from poles now made it safe to work around the aircraft. So, with three larger poles we made a tripod, which we centered over the engine of the airplane. To the apex of this tripod we fastened the chain block. We took the cowling off the machine over the engine, secured a good hitch on it with the chain and then we were ready to lift. Slowly, but surely, the aircraft came up, and soon we had it lifted free of the water!

At this stage we thought we had done about all we could do, until we had a new ski flown in and tools to straighten the wing. But we were stunned that no one had come to look for us. We thought the first trip by searchers would be a fellow pilot with a ski-equipped aircraft. There was a buddy system prevailing, which meant pilots would help each other out in circumstances like this. Since we were at our intended destination, the first plane in would find us. But not a sound was heard.

So we continued to work on the aircraft. The ski was made of aluminum alloy, with a flat ski runner, made stiff by a half-round housing riveted to the ski bottom. This housing, like a tunnel, flat on the bottom and rounded on top, had collapsed completely in the center of the ski. We now had two axes, since another one had been found among the guides' articles. We used one ax as a chisel and the other to pound it with, and cut off the rivets so the back half of the broken housing could be removed from the ski. A piece of wood was then pushed into the front of the tunnel, which kept the ski runner more or less flat.

We were now able to start the engine and taxi the plane back to the cabin. About this time it finally dawned on us that if nobody was coming for us, we just might be able to fly ourselves out! With the aircraft at the cabin it was certainly more convenient to work on it.

Milt set to work to get a permanent piece of wood whittled to just the right shape to pound in the tunnel on the front of the ski. When this was completed it again held the ski runner flat. In the meantime I took out the screws that held the skin over the end of the bent wing. By using poles pushed in from the open end of the wing we could gradually get it straightened. The ailerons are the moveable air foils at the outward end of each wing at the trailing edge.

They go up and down as the control column, or wheel, is moved from side to side, and this is what makes the aircraft bank. The wing tip that got bent crashing into the ice also bent the aileron enough that it would not move. Our straightening effort soon resulted in the ailerons again being able to move freely. Things were now really looking up, and finally we declared the aircraft in flying condition!

We had arrived at Toodoggone Lake on December 2. The morning of December 10 dawned clear with a nice bright sky, so we lost no time in getting ready to leave. Under normal, and legal, procedures, the major work we had done on the ski and wing would have been done by a qualified air engineer; he would then certify in the aircraft's logbook that the craft was airworthy. The aircraft would then be test flown to verify that it flew in a normal manner. If everything was satisfactory, it could then carry passengers. Of course, we didn't have an engineer to do the work or sign it out. We also agreed there would be no test flight. If we got off the lake, we were going! Later, when I reported the incident to the Department of Transport, I told the story exactly like it happened, because I knew that Des Murphy, the Superintendent of Air Regulations, would have done the same thing had it happened to him when he was bush flying!

We ended up taking with us some of the guides' very personal belongings that we had found in the snow—pictures, letters and diaries—which we later sent to them. We first had to taxi across the same bay we had broken through so that we could fill the aircraft with gas from the barrel left there. This time we knew exactly what the ice conditions were and we followed a proven route across the bay. We were off!

CHAPTER 4

The Rest of the Story

Take off from Toodoggone Lake with our patched up airplane was routine, and in the calm, clear air there wasn't a wiggle out of the aircraft. I had been quite concerned that the roughed-up wingtip may cause a vibration, but the aircraft flew completely normal.

With the type of conditions we were operating under there was no way to get any type of weather forecast. We had no inkling of what the weather may be like ahead of us. Since there was no such thing as small, portable AM receiving radios at that time, we didn't have a radio to hear public radio weather reports or news. Many bush flying operations were normally run by this method of not knowing what the weather ahead would be. Back then, there were many huge areas that had no weather reporting stations. In those cases, if the weather looked satisfactory at the point of departure the pilot just went. If he could get to his destination, fine. If the weather closed down he would just land somewhere in between, hopefully at a place that had some type of accommodation, like a cabin or, best of all, a trading post.

In hindsight, this type of operation looks hazardous…and it was. The most risky of all was the type we were on, where you just tell someone you should be home in X number of days! At the time it was common and nothing much was ever thought of it. One of the main reasons I did not make commercial flying a lifetime career was the fact that so many fellow pilots that I knew, and often shared an aircraft with, lost their lives in accidents. When I took my commercial pilot training in Vancouver there was only one other fellow taking the commercial course with me at the old, historic, Aero Club of B.C. We often flew together and we became friends. He was fatally injured in a crash about two years later.

In 1956 another instructor and I taught a class of about thirty students at a flying school in Prince George. The other instructor then went into helicopter flying, didn't like it too well, so he quit and went into a private business venture. That didn't work out, so he went back to helicopter flying. He, too, lost his life in his helicopter. Two other well-known, very experienced pilots working out of Prince George at the time, both of whom I had flown with, later lost their lives in separate accidents. I could go on and on, but one particular case remains riveted in my mind.

Bobby Deasum was a young pilot with a lot of flying experience, including flying in South America. He flew for a bush airline in B.C. for a while, then went to the provincial government that at the time was doing field work with bush-type aircraft. He told me he wanted to get out of commercial flying, and his reason for going to work for the government was that he was flying survey parties. He thought maybe he would get an opportunity to get into the surveying profession. But he said that didn't work out, plus they only flew in the summer and he couldn't stand being in Victoria all winter doing virtually nothing.

In early spring of 1955 he was back in Prince George, flying for a well-known bush airline, with a brand new Cessna 180 airplane. This was Cessna's latest model, highly advertised as a promising bush machine. Bob phoned me and said they had put skis on his new airplane. He said, "I've never flown on skis, you better come and check me out." I just laughed, because he had much more flying experience than I had, but I said I would be glad to ride with him while he checked himself out on skis. I did and we had a good time.

In the early summer he was at the coast flying the same aircraft, which was now on floats. One day he took off from Ocean Falls with three foresters to do a low-level reconnaissance flight over thick, large timber of the coastal rainforest. He was headed for a destination two hours away, but he never arrived.

A huge air search, which resulted in another crash and three or four more people losing their lives, failed to find any trace of the missing aircraft. To the best of my knowledge it has still never been found.

I have stated that I had a fairly active sixth sense. Also, in my life I have had the odd thing happen at night which is not a dream, but more like a vision. While we were at the cabin at Toodoggone Lake it happened again. One night from a sound sleep, Bobby Deasum was suddenly standing there by his wrecked airplane! He was in a hilly, old, logged over area of huge stumps and much undergrowth. Plain as anything he "said," "the engine quit cold, I didn't have a chance!" I remember being surprised that he was in an area that had once been logged, as everyone assumed he would be down in heavy, green timber. In my vision I tried to ask him where he was, but it all vanished just as quickly as it had appeared. I would be really shocked if someday they find the wrecked remains of the missing airplane in a logged-over, hilly area with large stumps!

That episode has forever haunted me. One reason is because of the circumstances. Aircraft engines were extremely reliable, but the Cessna 180 was accidentally designed with a flaw. I didn't know this at the time of my dream. It was later discovered that when a new machine had about 300 hours of heavy loaded flying and was under heavy load at the time, the engine could seize and abruptly stop due to one cylinder not getting proper cooling. Eventually, forced landings were happening all over the place until Cessna made the proper modifications. The plane that Bob had was one of the very first that was put into commercial use, as well as one of the first to reach 300 hours of tough flying. It was on floats and heavily loaded on a reasonably warm day, but the design fault was not yet known, and engine failure otherwise would have been very rare. Also, the expression, "the engine quit cold," would be the way a pilot would describe an engine failure due to it seizing up, as compared to fuel starvation, for example, where the engine would sputter along for a bit before stopping completely.

Oh yes, one other, maybe minor, reason that I quit flying was because it was gradually losing its sense of fun. Like so many things in life, it used to be so carefree and casual. There wasn't even a control tower at the Prince George airport while I was flying and when I took the training to get my instructors license at Kelowna, B.C., the airport was only a grass strip 1,700 feet long! Now, of course, that same airport is a very major, completely secured and controlled airport for big jets. At this time it is hard to imagine just how casual and carefree it once was to have been flying from such a facility.

It seemed like everybody knew everybody. I would call the Prince George radio range station on the radio, using the aircraft identification, and the operators would answer, calling me by my name. I, in turn, knew the operators and would return the call using their names! Not exactly proper protocol, but typical of the casual and friendly procedure used until about 1960.

At least once I was surprised at the extent that everybody really did know everybody. It was spring, with most of the snow gone. I was on skis, out somewhere southeast, and wanted to leave a passenger at Quesnel. I could see the snow was all gone at the Quesnel airport except for a long strip down the west side of the runway where they had blown the snow in the winter as they cleared the runway. I told the radio operator at Quesnel I was on skis and wanted to land. He told me I couldn't because the airport was closed for ski flying. I told him I could land on the snow strip. He answered, "Who's the pilot?" I told him and he was almost apologetic, "Oh, that's okay then, go ahead and land!" I had no idea that any radio operator at Quesnel had ever even heard of me! But here he had just stuck his neck out for me, giving me permission to land at a closed airport. Fortunately, I landed and took off again without incident.

Another time I wanted to fly south, this time in a wheel-equipped aircraft. I was in the weather office at Prince George, which was located on the second floor of the airport administration building. A line squall with roll-type clouds could easily be observed to the south, my intended route. The weather associated with this type of system can be a terror on light aircraft and from looking at it even the weather forecaster couldn't judge how severe it was. Then a Canadian Pacific Airlines flight came in, on its Whitehorse to Vancouver run, with the next stop being Quesnel. The captain and first officer came to the weather office. When they were leaving I asked the captain if he would make a judgment on the roll cloud when they went by it, to see if I could get past it. He said, "Sure, I'll do that." So I waited in the radio room for his report. A little later the captain called the Prince George radio range station to say that it looked okay for me to go. We thanked him and I went, with no trouble. Try that today! For starters the captain wouldn't dare do that, for fear I might crash, then he and his airline would be sued!

I had a personal, first-name relationship with some of the top personnel in the Department of Transport, the official body that governed flying. Desmond (Des) Murphy, the Superintendent of Air Regulations for the Pacific Division, had been an old-time bush pilot, then a test pilot in war time. It was common for him to fly to Prince George and I got to know him quite well. At our flying school we had a student, older than most, who was having trouble and we couldn't get him to the solo flying stage. One day the other instructor, who had more time instructing than I did, told me he was finished with this student. He said if it was okay with me, he was going to "wash him out," tell the Department of Transport that he couldn't make it and turn in his student permit. The main problem was the man was nervous and we couldn't get him over it.

I told the other instructor I would spend some more time with him before I gave up. Soon Des Murphy came to Prince George and I told him about our problem student. He said he used to teach flying as a sideline in the 1930s. He told me student nervousness was a common problem when he was instructing, so he informed me of some methods he had used to get them over it. Here was a type of challenge made to order for me, so I took the older student under my wing. When I felt he was getting near the solo stage, I decided to take him to Vanderhoof.

The airport at Vanderhoof had long, earth-surfaced runways, which are easier to land on than hard, tarmac-surfaced strips. Also, there was no traffic whatsoever at Vanderhoof and only a couple of families even living at the field, so there would be nothing to distract him. I told the other instructor to come in the other aircraft, if I wasn't back in three hours!

All the way there I talked about everything except flying, and I even took him down to look at two moose in a slough. It was a calm and relaxed student that arrived at Vanderhoof. He didn't know why we had gone to Vanderhoof, he thought it was just for some variety. But I soon sent him solo and he completed not one, but two, successful solo flights from the field! I continued with him right through until he received his private pilot's license along with the rest of the students. Des Murphy and another top Department of Transport official came to Prince George to present the new flyers with their licenses. No student was prouder of his achievement than was my special trainee that soloed in Vanderhoof! Okay, so I felt good, too, knowing the other instructor had given up on him. This fellow bought his own plane and flew it successfully for a number of years, all because of an exceptionally thoughtful and understanding public official in a high position, who knew how to act like a human being. Later, several of these new pilots went on to get a float-flying endorsement on their license and I did all this instruction

Des Murphy used to fly the government twin-engine aircraft when the Department of Transport officials came to Prince George. While having a casual conversation with him prior to his departure one day, he said to me, "You know, some people say when you get older you're not as safe a pilot, that you can't see as well." Then he continued, "But I think I'm safer than those young guys, although I might not see as well, I know exactly where to look and what to look for." I certainly agreed with him, but it sounded strange and refreshing coming from the Superintendent of Air Regulations. It was more like one pilot thoughtfully talking to another. Those were great, free and easy times.

Thirty minutes into our flight from Toodoggone Lake the little gremlins got in one more shot at us. The air was completely stable and the aircraft just sat in the sky as steadily as an easy chair sits on a livingroom floor. Suddenly, with no warning at all, the right wing, the one that was damaged when it hit the ice, just dropped! Quick application of hard left aileron and rudder brought it back to normal, so our fright was short lived and we could start breathing again! But in the instant when that side of the aircraft dropped away from us, I think we each sprouted a few gray hairs. The bit of turbulent air that caused the drop was actually an omen, a forerunner of deteriorating weather to come. The sky soon became overcast and the clouds were getting lower the further we progressed. We were thankful that the high mountains of the Russell Range, Bower Creek and the Upper Pelly River area were behind us while the weather was still relatively good. From the Lower Pelly we could cut corners to get into the Rocky Mountain Trench, north of Fort Graham.

The straight valley, with the Finlay River meandering down it, was a much better area to be flying in if the weather continued to deteriorate, and we had definitely flown into bad weather. Before getting to Finlay Forks it had started to snow. This required us to lower our altitude so the ground, or rather tree tops, could be seen through the falling snow. Of course, we debated landing at Finlay Forks. Here would be friendly people and a warm, pleasant place to stay. But there was no communication with the outside world and we thought for sure there would be search planes out looking for us, battling the same storm, so we really wanted to keep going until we arrived at some place from which we could radio or phone. Also, there was no landing area on the river marked by evergreens at Finlay Forks. Roy MacDougall would mark out a landing area each winter as soon as the ice was suitable. No little trees marking a landing strip meant he didn't consider the river ice suitable for an aircraft. Also, even if we took a chance and landed on the river, it would have been more difficult to land on the unbroken snow without the marker trees, because of the "white-out" condition. As well, we were worried about our repaired ski and we wanted to be near a road if possible, when we landed.

Therefore, we decided to overfly Finlay Forks and carry on to Fort McLeod. On the way north we had seen a runway, marked by good-sized evergreens, on McLeod Lake. Even in a white-out we could make a landing beside the markers. However, a short distance south of Finlay Forks we began to doubt our decision as the snowfall became heavier. We now had to decrease our altitude to just above the tree tops in order to see the ground. At this stage we also lowered the flaps to the 50 percent position and reduced speed, in order to increase maneuverability. (Flaps are air foils on the wings designed to be lowered part way for better lift and to allow the craft to fly a bit slower. Full extension of the flaps is usual for landing as it lowers the landing speed.)

Milt would call out the landmarks as we flew up the Parsnip River, so I would know where we were. He called out, "Just went by the big cabin," and I knew we had passed his old trapper's cabin at Scotts Creek. I was following every bend in the river in order to keep above it, in case a landing would be forced on us, for example, by encountering snow too thick to continue through. Soon Milt identified the Nation River. From there on were only insignificant landmarks until we reached the Pack River, where we would turn right and follow that waterway to Trout Lake, then to McLeod.

Milt Warren had limped back to England numerous times in badly shot-up bombers in World War Two, where he had completed a full tour of duty as a wireless air gunner. Maybe this kind of thing we were doing was no great deal to him. On the other hand maybe he was getting tired of this sort of escapade!

The heavy snow kept falling, but coming in over the mouth of the Pack River, just above the huge cottonwood trees, we could see the evergreens ahead marking a landing area. A smooth landing in the soft, deep snow beside the trees and the Toodoggone venture was over. I stayed at Fort McLeod in one of Justin McIntyre's cabins. Milt walked up to the highway, less than half a mile away, and was just in time to catch a bus to Prince George.

Later, when an air engineer examined our patched-up ski, he said it was probably stronger than the original! To this day I have the whittled-down spruce log that held the ski together. Just one of the mementos from the past.

Oh, yes, why didn't someone come looking for us? Well, when I had originally told my brother of our plans, I said we expected to be back in three or maybe four days. I also said we were taking food for ten days. So, when I asked the vital question my brother said, "Well, you said you were going for ten days!" I was not married then or things would have been different. Milt's wife kept phoning my brother, not thinking for a minute that we intended to be gone so long, but my brother kept assuring her! And no plans were in place to start a search the next day, either!

Oh well, when I quit flying I could sit back, put my feet up and proudly state that no one ever had to come looking for me. Also, our being stranded for so long without being searched for must be a Canadian record, if such records were kept. And speaking of records, here's one that I would bet on.

When I took my commercial training course at Sea Island Airport (now called Vancouver International) it was required that I get ten hours of night flying. The winter weather was bad night after night, preventing flying, and I was anxious to get the remainder of my solo night flying time in. Finally, the weather cleared and on February 8, 1953, I went out after supper in the pitch black in a Fleet 80 aircraft registered CF-ENC. I asked the instructor at the Aero Club of B.C., how long would the fuel in the tank last and his answer was, "A lot longer than you will". My mind said "challenge." So I started doing what are called circuits and bumps. This means that you take off, fly a rectangular circuit, then touch down, but before stopping you apply power and take off again. From one touch-down to the next takes about five minutes. I did this for exactly three hours straight!

The instructor had to stay around, so he went to the control tower and spent part of the time with the tower operator. I had to radio the tower traffic controller three different times for each circuit, to ask permission for each stage of the circuit, and the operator had to give me three clearances for each circuit, then I would acknowledge having heard each clearance. During the time I was flying there were other aircraft in the circuit. Another flying school had two, sometimes three, aircraft in the sky doing the same as I was. They were using faster Cessna aircraft and from time to time would pass me. As well, this was a busy airport, even then, so airliners were coming and going, but as it turned out there wasn't a single circuit where I had to go around again without landing, or delay, or anything else! We were all using the same runway, so what I am telling you, while the exact truth, is nothing short of miraculous. Yes, I'll bet on that three hours of straight, uninterrupted circuits and bumps at night, as being a Canadian record. Near the end I was getting so tired that when I picked up the microphone to talk, I could hardly remember what to say, even though it was the same thing over and over. My instructor was beginning to worry that I might use all the fuel after all!

CHAPTER 5

When They Don't Come Back

ith people and airplanes traveling constantly through wild and baron country, it was inevitable that sometimes one would fail to return on schedule. Some of these people could be considered lost, while some were just delayed. The trappers and prospectors who spent nearly all their time in the bush almost never got lost. Of course, if they did and had to spend an extra night or two in the bush, it would have been such an inconsequential event as to be not worth mentioning. It was usually the weekend hunters who got lost. Mostly they were not even lost, but if they were a few hours overdue someone always reported them as lost and a search would be mounted.

The first search I was involved with, in 1952, was also the most heart-rending of any that were to follow. An eleven-year-old boy was traveling with an older boy, by motorbike, on the trails of the old Yukon Telegraph Line between Blackwater and, of all places, Graveyard Lake. They had camped overnight, and in the morning the young boy went to get water from a creek and didn't come back.

I believe it was the next day before a full-scale search was started. And full-scale it was, with people turning out in great numbers. There was a line of men nearly a mile long, strung out side-by-side, close enough to each other as to always be able to see all the ground between the searchers. They had leaders stationed along the line to guide it. They would search straight into the bush for some miles, then return and search an area next to the previous line. One of the searchers was an old-time Indian tracker with tremendous skill. He ranged ahead of the other searchers looking for any sign. If somebody found anything suspicious they would call, relayed by each searcher in line, for the tracker to come.

At that time there was no racism whatsoever regarding the old-time Natives, with white people and Native Indians each respecting each other. The Native population was always referred to as Indians, without any disrespect intended. Nor was the term resented by the Indians, who also used the same word when referring to themselves. When a searcher required the tracker, he would call out, "Bring the Indian." This call would be repeated down the line of searchers until heard by the tracker. By the same token, the Indian tracker was the most popular person on the search, with everybody liking him and speaking highly of him. One day, when everyone seemed to need the tracker at the same time, he jokingly said to the searchers, "Bring Indian here, send Indian there, get Indian to end of line. Want Indian all over the place!" But his great skill in tracking, such as one time tracking down a wayward searcher, has been told and retold by many men who were on the search.

They searched again the area near where he had gone missing. On the re-search they often found little articles lost by the searchers, including a cigarette lighter. One man even claimed he lost a nickel and the tracker found it! The B.C. Forest Service set up a tent camp, including a cookhouse, right at the sight. It was a tremendous effort by a large segment of the local population. Probably the most amazing aspect of the whole thing was the fact there was no organized search and rescue organization, or even organized police involvement. If something had to be done during that period in history, people just did it and they didn't require any official to tell them what to do or how to do it. Also at that time, there were a great number of experienced bushmen and outdoors people in the area who came to help.

The late Walter Gill, a game inspector with the B.C. Game Department, called me to ask if I would fly on the search. With Walter as a spotter, we thoroughly covered the search area. A boy in a panic situation, such as being lost in those endless miles of bush, would be capable of traveling a very long distance. We therefore searched the bush a greater distance from the sight where he went missing, than was covered by the ground searchers. Mind you, some of the best bushmen and the tracker did venture far ahead, in a vain attempt to find any sign of him in case he did travel a long way.

We flew low over the trees, desperately looking for some indication of the lost boy. Any flash of a different color would get the adrenalin flowing, until it would be identified as a stump or maybe a patch of bunch grass. After flying for some time over the bush, we would again cover every little opening in case he heard us and was able to reach an opening. When we ran low on fuel, we would go to the Vanderhoof airport and get gas.

During the search a very large, old boar grizzly was located. It was shot and autopsied, but nothing whatsoever was found, so the old bear was presumed just to have been in the wrong place at the wrong time. Nevertheless, it was something that had to be done.

It was very sad to think a young boy, happy, healthy and having a great adventure, was going to perish in a harsh land of never-ending bush infested with mosquitoes and flies and harboring no end of scary noises at night. The second day the Royal Canadian Air Force sent in a twin-engine airplane to assist. But it had poor visibility for searching and was too fast to be of much use. They took one flight, then left after a short reconnaissance, leaving the flying to me, with Walter Gill as a spotter, in a Cessna 170. In spite of the best effort of so many capable, willing and highly skilled people, no trace was ever found of the missing boy. It was just like he had vanished into thin air.

I probably searched for ten or twelve lost people in the bush and this was the only time it ended with a fatality. I don't even remember the majority of those searches, but they were for missing hunters who often were not really lost. One thing I do remember is that not a single person that I searched for ever called to thank me! In one case a man we searched for strongly resented our looking for him!

Two game wardens walked across a frozen lake to investigate a complaint about a man who lived by himself in a cabin with no road access. It was spring and the ice on the lake was nearly ready to go out. The two wardens walked across the lake in the morning, when the ice was quite well frozen. They were at the cabin for some time, the sun shone brightly and the temperature rose. The wardens decided it was too dangerous to go back on the ice, so they elected to walk around the lake to get back to their vehicle.

When they didn't get back that night, Walter Gill, their boss, called me to look for them. When we saw the vehicle where they had left it, the concern greatly increased. We flew over the lake, searching intensely for any telltale hole in the ice. But the ice was so rotten, with various openings, that we couldn't be sure. From the air we couldn't see anything amiss at the cabin, so we went home and Walter prepared to organize a search party.

The walking around the lake was really tough going. It was a maze of willows and alders, often knee-deep in water. The men didn't have food with them and it became apparent they would have to spend the night in the bush. Game wardens didn't normally carry handguns, but one warden had been in the B.C. police and still had a revolver, which he had with him. Near evening they saw some grouse and the warden said he would shoot a couple to eat. The other game warden, the near legendary Alf Janke, was senior and he said, "No, don't shoot them, the season is closed." The other warden said he was hungry and was going to shoot one, which he did.

Alf Janke was so angry that he made his own fire to sit around at night, away from the warden who had cooked and eaten his grouse! Before a search got started, the two arrived home not even speaking to each other. And when the senior warden found out his boss had searched for him from the air, then arranged a ground search for the next day, he was furious. He was a bushman, having been a northern trapper before joining the department. He said no one had to come looking for him, and he thought his boss should have known that!

In another case, I was later furious at a missing hunter! One year in November a very, very cold snap settled in over the Prince George area. The temperature dropped to about thirty degrees below zero Fahrenheit at night and warmed only very little in the day. On top of that, the wind blew strong and straight out of the north. And if that wasn't enough, it was overcast with solid cloud, completely blotting out the sun. A hunter failed to return from a daytrip near the Blackwater Road. Terry Hammond, who at the time was editor of the *Prince George Citizen*, phoned me to ask if I would fly a search. The early, severe cold had caught aircraft usually available for a search, still on floats. The only aircraft available for us was a Piper Cub! No other aircraft was less suitable for severe cold weather operation than it. To this day I really can't believe I did it, but Terry Hammond talked me into flying the aircraft, saying we may be able to save a life, and he went along as a spotter. Terry had been a pilot in WW II, so he, too, knew what we were up against.

It was impossible to shield the engine cylinders of the Piper

The broad valley of the Finlay River near the trading post of Finlay Forks.

CF-GIM on the late winter snow at Finlay Forks.

The author emerges from a fly-in tent camp. Two foresters would live in this for a week or more before being flown out by the author.

Above: Milt Warren at one of our winter prospecting camps and in his underwear cooking breakfast *(right).*

John Hallam, in hat, and Drew Gray ready to be flown out of a wilderness summer camp.

The author relaxing at night at a winter prospecting site. *Photo: Milt Warren*

Marge and Roy MacDougall with Margie and the dog, Pete. *Photo: Marge Donovan collection*

Above, from left: Art Van Somer, trappers Mort Tier and Ed Strandberg, the MacDougalls and Little Marge, trapper Ludwig Smaaster and Alan Patterson, son of author R. M. Patterson, with rear view of Finlay Forks store. *Photo: Marge Donovan collection*

Right: Two trappers constructing an elaborate, high cache, using a rickety ladder. Their names are lost to history. *Photo: Marge Donovan collection*

A very rare, old photograph of Fort Graham. The riverbank gradually eroded away until the flood of 1948 partially washed it out from under the buildings. The dog sleighs appear to be loaded with baled fur. *Photo: Marge Donovan collection*

Splendid-looking sleigh dogs belonging to a Native man at Fort Ware, circa 1954.

In 1954 Harvey Charlie poses for the author in front of his new cabin at Fort Ware. He wanted his wife in the picture, but she wouldn't come out. Harvey died in the mid-1980s, but his brother Antoine is considered to be the last of the old-time trappers, spending most of his time at his line on the Fox River.

A cabin at old Fort Ware. There were a few cabins and only the abandoned HBC store at Ware in 1955.

Above: The desolate beauty of our snowshoe trail in the wilderness of the north, 150 miles from any road.

Right: Milt Warren breaking snowshoe trail through the snow-laden bush.

Aircraft on the river ice at Fort Ware. Note the open hole of water.

The aircraft at a winter prospecting camp.

Forester Bob Darnall cooking a meal at one of our summer camps.

Bob Darnall admiring the scenery at one of our wilderness camps.

Loading up the Cessna at the Prince George airport for a winter trip north.

The log building that housed the Fort McLeod trading post for many years. This photo was taken in 1992, about 30 years after it closed as a historic store.

Justin McIntyre posing behind the counter of his Fort McLeod trading post.

Justin McIntyre serving a customer at his Fort McLeod trading post. Note the postal scales in the little cage on the left. His gold scales, used for purchasing placer gold, were also in this cage.

A typical high mountain lake.

One of the many small, pretty lakes we often flew in and out of.

The author with Jack Mitchell's dog, which just loved to fly. Of course, the alternative for the dog was to carry a pack on the wilderness trips to and from Fort McLeod. *Photo: Jack Mitchell*

The Super Cub at Pine Pass.

One way to warm the engine in cold weather! Nothing like putting a stove under it and getting a fire going.

A trapper's cabin in the shadows of a winter afternoon.

Milt Warren at the cabin on Two Brothers Lake.

Milt and the Caterpillar tractor that was flown to Two Brothers Lake in pieces and then reassembled. We were on our way to the old mine camp, so Milt had on his ever-present Trapper Nelson packboard. It held emergency supplies and equipment, including his trusty 30-30 rifle in its laced buckskin sheath. The ax in his hand was vital if forced to spend a night in the bush.

Examining the shovel we used to replace the tail ski, before the aircraft went through the ice. *Photo: Milt Warren*

Shortly after the aircraft went through the ice. We are gathering poles to make an ice bridge.

The tripod assembled and chain hoist hooked up, in preparation for lifting the aircraft from the ice.

Milt chopping the tail assembly out of the ice, in preparation for lifting.

The author guides the broken ski through the ice as the aircraft is hoisted from the lake. Note the bent wing tip. *Photo: Milt Warren*

With the craft clear of the ice, the broken ski can be clearly seen.

Just another mountain out there somewhere!

A pretty lake in the Chilcotin area of westcentral B.C.

The Prince George airport as it appeared in the early 1950s.

Approaching Great Beaver Lake many years before there was road anywhere near it.

A rare photo of seven wolves on Great Beaver Lake. They had earlier killed and eaten a moose. They returned to the kill after a light snow had fallen. The kill was just above the center wolf where the tracks are concentrated. The author, alone in the aircraft, managed to operate both the camera and plane without even flying into the frozen lake!

Herd of caribou cows, calves and one bull in the alpine, with first fall of snow at the high altitude. Larry de Grace, manager of Industrial Forestry Service Ltd., took the picture while the author positioned the aircraft.

Loading wolf bait from the game warden's truck at Vanderhoof Airport.

Ray Baynes and Carl Hagen, in hat, enjoying the quiet tranquility of Germansen Lake.

The old, historic seaplane base in South Fort George at the foot of Hamilton Street in its zenith hour, showing eight floatplanes at rest, circa 1958.

The ill-fated Stranraer aircraft that ended its career in a fiery crash east of Quesnel was either this one or its sister ship. Photo was taken at Sea Island Airport, now Vancouver International.

Above: Junkers CF-ABK on the river at Fort Ware was purchased on May 14, 1929, by Canadian Airways of Winnipeg and was taken out of service in 1940. Evidence indicates this photo was taken early in its career. *Photo: Marge Donovan collection*

Inset: This is Junkers 34, CF-ATF, prior to take-off from the Fraser River at Prince George in 1962 on its way to the aviation museum in Ottawa. That was the last flight of any Junkers in Canada. It was purchased new in 1932 and extensively flew the northern Canadian wilderness skies until 1960.

The Manson Creek trading post in 1979, looking very little different than it did when first viewed by the author in 1948.

The post at Takla Landing still in use by the HBC in 1958. The author slept in the porch for a few nights.

Herb Cooke at the motor in his riverboat, with Henry Hobe in the bow. The old motor visible in the water is the engine from the historic car that was dragged through Monkman Pass in the 1930s.

Ferry Strobl is seen reading on the porch of Cooke and Hobe's main cabin on Herrick Creek.

Pretty rock and water formations in Monkman Pass area.

Above: Bob Darnall at one of Hobe's less-luxurious cabins on Herrick Creek. Much of the untidy yard is due to hunters and others camping there.

Left inset: Another of Hobe's cabins on the creek.

Unusual mountain formation east of Chesterfield Lake.

A new log cabin built by Carl Hagen at his little resort on Germansen Lake. The author, fisheries biologist Charlie Lyons and game biologist Ray Baynes were its first occupants.

Our 1955 camp at Fern Lake in northeastern B.C.

The remains of the historic car that was pulled through Monkman Pass as a publicity stunt. It rests on the banks of Herrick Creek near Herb Cooke's cabin, as seen in 1958.

Pan Phillips with his wife and young son outside their house at home ranch. Pan was featured in Rich Hobson's famous book *Grass Beyond the Mountains* and other books.

The ranch and other buildings of the Pan Phillips home ranch, circa 1958.

Right: The church at Kluskus Lake, showing the bell the author rang to impress his new girlfriend.

Below: Inside the old church at the abandoned Indian village of Kluskus.

The author fishing in the Blackwater River, about 1954.

In the year 2002 the author is still making coffee in a blackened pail over a campfire.

from the extreme cold and there was no heat, whatsoever, in the interior of the aircraft. The engine ran okay on the ground, so we decided to try a test flight. Take-off, climb and level flight was normal. But I knew that if the throttle was closed in the air, as for a normal glide prior to landing, the engine would quit! To come down one had to reduce power only part way to keep the engine firing so it wouldn't stop. On landing an aircraft like this the throttle has to be closed. So when we were near the ground and within range of the runway, I closed the throttle. Sure enough, the engine immediately stopped and I made a "dead-stick" landing. (When an engine stops in flight the resulting landing is called a dead-stick landing because no power is available to assist in landing if it is required.) The aircraft had no battery or electricity of any type, so Terry got out, in his great bundle of winter clothes, and pulled the propeller to turn the engine until it started.

Another feature was its short time of fuel duration, less than two hours, or even less than half that of most aircraft. In spite of all the handicaps, we loaded an extra can of gas in the rear, put on our warmest of winter wear and took off.

We went to the place on the Blackwater Road where he was supposed to be lost, where the ground searchers were working from, and started searching. There was a little snow on the ground, none in the trees due to the wind, so I had high hopes of at least finding his tracks. When our fuel run low we went to the nearest lake, landed on the ice and put our gas in the tank. Of course, the engine quit on landing. Only this time we had some difficulty in getting it started, due to the elapsed time it was sitting in the severely cold wind while we put the gas in the tank. It also quit a time or two more before we got into position for take-off. We went back searching over the tall trees and when next the fuel ran low we went home, agreeing we had given it our best shot. Since we had seen no sign of a fire, we figured he must have been unable to light one, and if this was the case, he most likely had perished.

The same weather pattern continued throughout the next day, but the morning of the following day dawned clear and quiet. Near noon the word came that the hunter had walked from the bush! What happened was he went hunting fifteen miles from where he was supposed to have been and where the search was being carried on! When he became lost, he made a fire and stayed there until the sun shone. When the sun came out he walked east and came to the road in twenty minutes. If he had used one iota of common sense, he would have known a bitter cold wind like we had could only have come from the north, thereby giving a sure-fire indication of directions. Or he could have used the wind as a guide, it never varied in direction, walked in a straight line for an hour or so, and if nothing turned up, could have retraced his steps to his camp. After two or three tries he would have been sure to find the road, the first day.

A person lost has a responsibility. People were risking their lives for him and he was making a fool of us. To add insult to injury, he had a long interview with the local radio station in which he did nothing but boast about his great bushmanship! He said he was so smart to have waited until the sun shone, so he knew which direction to go. This may have been what they did in Europe, but it certainly didn't go over here. He never had one word to say to, or about, all the searchers who were looking for him in the bitter winter weather. These searchers were all, at the least, giving up their time, losing income and, yes, taking great risk of injury. I never searched for another lost hunter.

When airplanes are missing it is a different story. Firstly, you know it has the potential to be dead serious and, secondly, you immediately think of all the places where you could have got into trouble and how you would want someone to look for you. Also, there is a definite camaraderie among pilots. So, with a, "Thank goodness it's not me," you get right at searching.

I've helped search for aircraft that, when found, had no survivors, as well as aircraft that were never found. I've also had searches that ended happily, including one that had a rather amusing climax, as well as one minor search where the "lost" pilot was anything but welcomed with open arms after he returned. I have said there was great comradeship among pilots, but I should have added the word "usually."

One Monday morning I got a call from the RCMP saying a plane was missing and asking whether I could take a look for it. A pilot, who was a stranger to the area, had flown up from the coast to Prince George. The next day he filed a flight plan to Fort St. James with a planned return later the same afternoon, when he would close the flight plan. When the police called they said the Department of

Transport reported the plane had not returned to Prince George. It had arrived in Fort St. James, so it went missing on the return flight.

At that time it was common practice for the Department of Transport to conduct a preliminary look for an overdue aircraft before calling in the RCAF, the region's official search group. That was why the police called me. The missing aircraft was a Seabee, an amphibious type capable of landing on either land or water. However, on this particular machine the wheels had been removed, making it a water machine only, and there were two people on board. It was midsummer, the weather was excellent and the flight was only fifty minutes each way, and there were several lakes en route suitable for the Seabee to land on. It seemed strange that much could go wrong, but when you are officially asked to search for a missing aircraft, you go.

I flew a floatplane with a couple of observers on a return trip over the route, checking out the lakes to see if the missing craft had landed on the water, as well as scanning the bush. A search for an aircraft requires constant staring at the ground by pilot and observers. You are looking for that telltale sign of a broken tree, or trees, or maybe a brief glimpse of something shining or off color. Often, an aircraft that has crashed in the bush has very little, or any, of the actual aircraft visible from the air, making it extremely difficult to see. Sometimes a wreck is spotted from the air, but proves hard to relocate later.

When I returned to Prince George to land on the Fraser River, I saw the missing Seabee tied to the dock! By the time I landed and got our aircraft tied up, the pilot of the Seabee was leaving. I got one glimpse of the pilot, who had a stupid look on his face, and I was really wondering what was going on. Then I saw the passenger; a real-life, walking Barbie doll, who should have been at her job of adorning the sales counter at a local pharmacy store!

The flying fraternity was pretty upset. A missing aircraft is a serious event and no one should ever, ever deliberately cause a false alarm resulting in a search. The pilot could have altered his flight plan by phone from Fort St. James saying he would be another day. Or, even if they got the amorous thoughts on the way back to Prince George, he could have first flown close enough to allow his short-range radio to contact Prince George. He should have done anything except cause a false alarm.

An hour later the Seabee left Prince George. I imagine the pilot got a blistering going over from Des Murphy, who was the Superintendent of Air Regulations at the Department of Transport. Oh yes, the police were not finished with their involvement in the affair, either. One of them later married the girl!

The easiest genuine search I was ever on occurred one fine summer day. In the early evening I got a call that a local, low-time private pilot and a passenger had left in the morning to a lake to fish and didn't return at the expected time. I went and arrived at the lake in thirty-five minutes. I immediately saw an SOS, marked with tree boughs, as well as some other ground-to-air signs. Beside the signs were two men, waving at me. I landed and picked them up. Their aircraft was also an amphibious Seabee. After taking off from the airport at Prince George, the pilot had forgotten to retract the wheels. When they landed on the lake with the under carriage in the down position, the aircraft immediately flipped over and sank. Fortunately, the two occupants were able to get to shore. Interestingly, to the best of my knowledge the aircraft was never located in the lake, which was only about four miles long.

On the ride home, the pilot sat in the front with me, while the passenger sat in the rear. I have never had a passenger so nervous. No, he was far beyond nervous, he was scared out of his wits. As we were losing altitude on the approach to landing at Prince George his actions intensified. He was moving all around, swinging his arms and jabbering away, somewhat incoherently. The lower our altitude, the worse he became. Just before landing on the Fraser River, I actually was quite concerned that he might panic. It was scary having someone like that sitting behind me, not knowing what he might do.

I saw another case showing the after-effects of a crash on the occupants. Pacific Western Airlines had a helicopter working out of an oil exploration camp on Stoney Lake near the Alberta border. In the morning, while some twenty miles away from the camp, it was taking off from a site, but wouldn't climb. It then settled down into a poplar forest. The helicopter was completely wrecked. Fortunately, neither the pilot nor engineer aboard was injured. Amazingly, the chopper's radio still worked, allowing the crew to contact their base, tell what had happened and state they would walk to camp at Stoney Lake.

The company sent a supervising engineer from Vancouver, who

came to Prince George on the regular airline, and that evening I flew him to Stoney Lake. We landed on the lake and were just walking the short distance to the camp, when the two men from the helicopter crash arrived exactly at the same time we did. It was twelve hours and twenty hard miles of walking since their crash, but they, especially the pilot, were still talking at a mile-a-minute. The engineer I brought in had trouble getting them slowed down enough so he could understand what they were saying about the crash!

Bad weather is by far the greatest cause of light aircraft getting into trouble. Almost all light aircraft and all bush flying operate under visual flight rules (VFR). This means the pilot must be able to see the ground at all times. To be legally permitted to fly in cloud, called instrument flight rules (IFR), the aircraft must have certain flight instruments not compulsory for VFR flying. Also, and most importantly, the pilot must have an instrument flight rating. This requires extensive, advanced flying training and annual tests to obtain and maintain the license. When a noninstrument-trained pilot, even a very experienced VFR pilot, gets into solid cloud, which gives the impression of being submerged in a bowl of milk, he or she can not keep the aircraft flying in a normal manner. Many tests have been carried out over the years and the average length of time a VFR pilot can fly blind, that is in cloud or other condition, unable to see anything except the instruments in front of him or her, before control is lost, is about ninety seconds! That's right, one and a half minutes in cloud and control is lost, which usually results in a high-speed, spiral dive. When this is for real with no instructor or check pilot to correct it, the aircraft hits the ground at a steep angle at high speed. Very seldom does anyone survive such a crash.

When flying visually, one must stay below the cloud cover. On a cross-country flight with deteriorating weather, the cloud base often keeps getting lower, resulting in the pilot having to fly ever nearer to the ground to keep below the cloud. Then there comes a point where there is not sufficient room above the ground to allow the pilot to fly any lower! In such a case, one of two things should be done: either turn back to point of departure or land the aircraft if there is somewhere to make a safe landing. And this decision should be made well before the weather becomes too severe. Too often a pilot with no instrument training has elected to fly into the cloud, almost always resulting in a fatal crash.

There was a very painful and vivid example of what happens when pilots not trained for instrument flying venture into the clouds, demonstrated in northern B.C. some years ago. Trevor Grimshaw, now living in Salmon Arm, had a long, illustrious career in flying in the north. One day he was flying his helicopter south toward Fort St. John in poor weather, when he heard on his radio the pilots of two Cessna aircraft talking. They were flying north down a valley, which turned out to be a branch of the Beaton, when low cloud shut off their route. They turned back, but clouds had also closed the route behind them, trapping them in the valley. Trevor was returning north from Fort St. John about an hour and a half later, when he heard them call "Mayday," the distress signal. He talked to them on the radio and one pilot said he was running low on gas and was going to take to the clouds to get out. Trevor told them not to enter the clouds, but instead to fly as slow as they could over the fairly small trees with their flaps fully down and just mush into the trees. They could have hit the trees as slow as about fifty miles per hour. Instead, they took to the clouds. Trevor heard the signal from one of them pushing the microphone button to talk, but nothing was said. Then, boom, he actually heard the crash on the radio, followed by silence.

Trevor Grimshaw radioed out to the authorities and then flew to where he was pretty sure they would be. The weather soon cleared and he found the wrecks. The aircraft were only a short distance apart and each had hit the swampy ground while going down at a very steep angle. There were two men and two women in each air-craft and, of course, there were no survivors. The airspeed indicators were stuck at the speed they hit the ground and going from memory Trevor thinks the indicators showed the speed at 240 mph for one and 260 mph for the other. The occupants were a flying farmers group from the United States and most likely would have walked away from a controlled landing in the trees had they only listened to an experienced pilot.

In mountainous country, like most of British Columbia, pilots flying visual in poor weather usually follow valleys. This is because the valley, the watershed of a creek or river, has a more level terrain than would be encountered while crossing watersheds, for example. The hazards of this include the danger, if following the valley upstream, of the valley floor rising until there is no room to keep flying under the clouds or space to turn around in! Pilots who were familiar with such things, would always fly close to one edge of a valley under such circumstances, in order to have the entire valley available for the turn. Unless the wind was wrong, it was usual to fly on the right-hand side of the valley for two reasons. Firstly, with the direction of rotation of most aircraft engines, it is quicker to turn to the left with a single-engine aircraft than it is to turn to the right. Secondly, the pilot is commonly sitting on the left side; thus, the terrain to the left is easier to see and evaluate. To avoid becoming another statistic and being listed in the obituary column, the pilot should closely watch the valley to his left and do a 180-degree turn before the valley becomes too narrow!

Several things should be taken into consideration in evaluating when to turn back. Each pilot must know the capabilities of the aircraft under the existing conditions and, very importantly, his own ability to achieve the expected results from the aircraft! Of course, a safety factor must be thrown in remembering that Mother Nature might toss a curve, such as an eagle appearing in your turning circle or, more likely, a vagrant gust of wind occurring to push you closer to the cliffs or bush.

Also, in low cloud and probably poor visibility in rain or snow, there is a danger of turning into a wrong valley unless the pilot is very familiar with the country. Turning upstream into a wrong creek valley could result in being faced with a mountain cliff-face ahead and no room for turning back! And sometimes even the veteran pilots make mistakes. About the time I started flying, a real old-time bush pilot in the Yukon was killed. The summary of the accident stated he had mistakenly turned up-stream in a mountain valley in bad weather. That really shook me up.

A point of interest here, the methods of flying visual in poor weather as just described has not changed one iota since the first bush pilots started opening up the north in the mid-1920s! All of the modern electronic equipment coming into use in recent years is of no use whatsoever for a VFR pilot flying down a valley under low clouds! Nor are modern aircraft any safer or more suitable for this type of operation than were most of the planes of the 1930s or even some from the late twenties. Many people who know nothing about the subject find this hard to believe, but it is the truth. The only difference is in the event of a crash, an electronic beeper may now indicate the position of the wreck, hopefully enabling it to be quickly found. In the searches described in this article there were no automatic electronic signaling devices available.

Common sense dictates that if a pilot does much flying, he will at times be forced to turn back because of bad weather. Yet, there have been pilots who bragged about never turning back. This was meant to imply they were somehow superior to other normal pilots who, from time to time, would have to beat a retreat back to the starting base. One private pilot boasted that he had made forty, or some such number, trips between Vancouver and a central interior town and never turned back once.

One fall day when the entire central interior of the province was blanketed with thick, low cloud, accompanied by much heavy rain, he took off from Vancouver with his wife and another couple aboard, bound for the interior. They were in a four-place aircraft (designed for four people) that retracted its wheels and went quite fast. When he didn't arrive, a search was started. I joined the search and on the third day, with an observer, was searching an area west of the Fraser River and south of Empire Valley. Word came on our radio that the Airforce Search and Rescue had found the airplane on Churn Creek. Since that was pretty close to our route back to Prince George, we went to the reported crash sight but climbed to high altitude so as not to interfere with rescue operations.

The wreck was in a deep, narrow valley near a tiny meadow that was too small to land a helicopter in. A Dakota transport plane, with the door off and paratroopers standing near, was circling over and over the sight. After dropping two or three drones to test wind conditions, a parachutist jumped. If ever my heart was in my mouth, this was it! The jumper floated down a good thousand feet and then had to go really close to a sheer cliff, five hundred feet straight up. The chute was so close to the rock face that we thought it might drift into the solid wall. But the chute settled down between the trees, right in the tiny opening! Because of the terrain the Airforce Dakota couldn't get any lower. Then two more rescuers jumped, having to endure the same death-defying conditions by the dangerous cliff face. They cut trees down, allowing a helicopter to land and bring out the bodies.

Churn Creek rises on the west side of French Mountain, flows first west, then north, before turning northeast to the Fraser River. The wreck was almost at the extreme headwaters of Churn Creek, in very steep terrain, giving every indication the pilot had been flying upstream, instead of downstream and probable safety. Had he been flying downstream, he would have been over ever-lowering terrain and eventually reached the Fraser River. The aircraft had hit the ground in a steep angle at very high speed, resulting in instant death for the occupants. Unfortunately, the pilot kept his record intact—he never turned back.

There is another type of accident involving mountain flying that, regrettably, occurs too often. The accident happens when an aircraft tries to fly over a mountain by going up a valley on the side of the mountain. Mountains are often steeper than they appear to be, with the result being the aircraft cannot climb fast enough to make it over the top. By the time the pilot realizes the aircraft will not make it, there is no room to turn back, because the pilot has been flying up a valley.

Usually, the pilots who make this deadly error in judgment are people who are completely unfamiliar with mountain flying. There is a mountain just west of the Penticton airport, in the British Columbia southern interior, that has had several accidents in the same valley. What has happened in the past is an aircraft came from the prairie, gassed up at Penticton, and then took off. It has always happened with crystal clear summer conditions accompanied by very hot weather. In the clear weather the pilot has headed straight west, intending to go over the innocent-looking, wooded mountain. The aircraft is now full of fuel and probably at, or near, all-up weight. Heat greatly decreases the climbing performance of an airplane, which results in the aircraft being unable to clear the mountain; thus, it crashes. Going from memory, I can recall at least two cases where the aircraft burned, each time with fatal results for a family. I know there has been more than two, but I can't recall other circumstances. All this happened in the same valley on the same mountain!

Another time, two prospectors were using a float-equipped aircraft in the rugged country near Telegraph Creek in northern B.C. They wanted to look at the prospecting possibilities in a valley on the side of a mountain. They went to inspect the mountain by flying UP the valley. It was a good performing aircraft they had, but it could not climb fast enough in the thinner air of higher altitude to clear the mountain. Again, by memory, I believe the crash was fatal.

After the wreck was found, another private pilot, with exactly the same type of aircraft, took a friend and went to see the crash. As incredible as it sounds, the second aircraft flew UP the valley to look for the wrecked airplane. The second aircraft, also, could not out-climb the mountain. It, too, crashed very close to the first one! As I remember, the two men survived this one.

It is a terrible and stupid mistake to try to fly over a mountain by way of a valley, no matter how innocent the sloping valley looks. Any experienced mountain pilot, or indeed any one with common sense, who wanted to inspect a valley on a mountainside would fly down the valley or across it, but never up it. A pilot wanting to fly over a mountain should make sure he or she is higher than the mountain before they commit themselves to crossing it. People familiar with mountains know there is often a downdraft encountered close to the mountain.

Different areas of the country have different peculiarities that affect flying. I learned to fly in Calgary, Alberta, and in that locality a major hazard for new pilots was (is) the wind. When we were going solo the instructor would caution us to come right back to the airport if the wind got up. I don't know how a junior pilot would judge the wind now, but in 1949, the instructor would tell us to watch the clothes on the clotheslines to see how far they were being blown and to see how fast the windmills were turning! (In those days, most farmers still had windmills to pump water for their horses and cattle.) I hope they don't have to rely on those two methods now, yet when you think about it, we were being taught to use a good deal of judgment. Inexperienced pilots from the prairie with no mountain experience intending to fly to the coast should first contact a flying school in a mountainous area to get some basic information on this type of flying.

When a person is with people, talking with them, and then watches them get into an aircraft and fly away never to be seen again, it certainly makes an impact on one's sense of mortality. Such a scene is still strongly impressed in my mind, though it happened about 1950. I was at the Prince George airport when a U.S.-registered airplane arrived. It was a Cessna Crane, a light twin-engine craft used extensively for advanced training purposes in WW II. Aboard it were two very jolly gentlemen, each about sixty years old. It was well on in the fall of the year and these two were away on sight-seeing trip in the north, obviously having a whale of a good time. To add to the happy-go-lucky atmosphere of the two was the fact they were dressed, and looked, exactly like they had intended to start up the John Deere and go plowing but suddenly decided to go on a trip instead. The scene would have made a first-rate subject for a Norman Rockwell painting.

I was with the gas attendant at the airport when he fuelled their aircraft. Because the Cessna Crane had notoriously poor performance on one engine, they had stripped the machine of as much weight as possible, including the battery and electrical system (a great convenience but not required for VFR flying, as they are used to operate radios and modern navigation systems). Thus, the gas attendant had to pull the propellers for them to start the engines. With happy smiles and friendly waves, they were gone.

They went to Grande Prairie, Alberta, started for Edmonton, but never arrived. At that time there was no direct highway between Grande Prairie and Edmonton; it was a long stretch of bush and undulating hills with almost no distinguishing landmarks. This was part of what was known as the Northwest Staging Route, the airway from Edmonton to Fairbanks, Alaska. Thousands of aircraft were ferried over this route during wartime; large numbers of civilian aircraft also used the route after the war. For some reason, more aircraft went missing on this most southerly section of the route, between Edmonton and Grande Prairie, than on any of the northern sections. An immense search failed to find the missing Cessna.

Then a strange thing happened. Several years later, a Canadian Pacific DC3 airliner was flying the airway from Grande Prairie to Edmonton, as they did every day. On this trip the co-pilot looked out his window, then said, "There's a crashed airplane." Sure enough, it turned out to be the missing Cessna Crane! That was one of the most mysterious events regarding lost aircraft that has ever been recorded. Thousands of flights had been made over the crash without it being seen, and then one day it "appeared."

The cause of the crash was eventually determined. The weather had not been good. There had been rain with danger of freezing rain. When an aircraft flies in rain when the temperature is at, or just slightly below, the freezing mark, ice forms on the wings. It forms on the leading edge of the wings, and as ice builds up it destroys the lift of the wing. Ice can form rapidly. An aircraft can only fly about six minutes in freezing rain before the built-up ice will so deteriorate the lift of the wing that the aircraft can no longer fly. As the lift of the wing deteriorates, ever more speed is required to keep it flying. Finally, its maximum speed in level flight will no longer sustain it in the air and it just sinks to the ground at high speed. This was the case with the Cessna.

The direction of the crash was opposite to their intended direction of travel, indicating they had turned around and were trying to get back to Grande Prairie. If the temperature had risen to just one degree above the freezing mark, it would have quickly melted the ice. But, it didn't. The aircraft went into the bush at a very high rate of speed. It was just a heap of mangled metal at the end of a long stretch of broken bush. Why no searcher, or casual observer in the air, saw that swath of broken trees remains one of the great mysteries of northern flying. Not that it would have mattered to the occupants, who had been killed on impact.

The aviation weather system prevailing at the time consisted of eleven forecast stations in Canada and hundreds of weather reporting stations. Weather observers took the readings at each station hourly, then distributed it to all stations in the region by teletype. When a pilot went into a weather station to see what the weather was like in an area, they were given this readout of the existing weather at the stations in the region. The only problem was that most private pilots couldn't understand it, because it was all in code. Thus, they required interpretation, usually accompanied by a briefing.

Weather observers were on duty at all major weather stations, twenty-four hours a day. At the eleven forecast offices in Canada, which included Prince George, forecasters were on duty just during regular working-day hours, including weekends. In the common-sense era of the 1950s, observers would interpret the weather for the pilots and usually give advice to pilots who could not read the teletype sheets. Even after I had learned all the codes, I counted heavily on further advice the weather observers would give me. They knew far more about the weather than I did, so I never once went against their advice or doubted their opinions. I can certainly think of cases where I was glad I had listened to them, and I can't think of a single case of being given poor advice.

However, the wise people of our modern world then ruled that weather observers must not give advice to, or even interpret information for, pilots. And, as we have pointed out, there were only observers available at the vast majority of weather offices. This lofty chore of giving information to pilots was then reserved for the highly trained weather forecasters only. The lowly observer then simply handed the pilot a sheet of paper. Never mind if the pilots who needed the information most were unable to make any sense of all the vital information encoded on the paper. Alas, everything has changed. The weather offices are now gone from the airports, and the pilots get the information electronically and never talk to anyone.

One time I was at the Prince George weather office when there was no forecaster on duty, just an observer. I knew all the personnel there and often just dropped in to visit. Like most of the observers, this person was very knowledgeable about the subject. Again, a U.S. light aircraft came along and the two men from it came to the weather office. This was their first trip north and they were headed for Alaska. There were very poor weather conditions existing over almost all of Central and Northern B.C. The meteorological observer explained how cold, moist, unstable air with low cloud and many heavy storm cells prevailed throughout most of their intended route and he suggested they should stay at Prince George until the weather improved.

They wouldn't listen to him. The observer became insistent, too, because as they talked, he discovered they were inexperienced as well as unfamiliar with the country. They were completely unfamiliar with the vast, vacant, mountainous north, with its endless miles of bush, rivers and wooded hills. To top it off, their aircraft was wheel equipped—a real problem when airports could be 150 miles or more apart. The observer went well beyond what he had to in advising them, since he knew they were taking a terrible chance if they went. Finally, when there was no stopping them and they were leaving, his parting words were, "What are your favorite flowers?"

When they left, he looked at me and said, "That was an awful thing I said to them wasn't it?" Awful or not, it soon proved to be a correct remark. They were both killed in a crash on their way to Fort Nelson. I've often wondered what their final thoughts were just before they crashed.

I have searched for lost airplanes, other than those documented here, including at least one that was never found. However, I will tell about just one more search, as it had a rather unique ending. A prominent Prince George business man, who had been a bomber pilot in the war, started to fly again and purchased a Cessna 170 in Vancouver. He and his wife filed a nonstop flight plan to Prince George but didn't arrive. It was well into March of an early spring and the snow had undergone much thawing, had settled and then refroze.

The Royal Canadian Airforce Search and Rescue unit made Prince George the search headquarters. At that time they allowed experienced civilian pilots to officially search with them, allotting them a quadrant to cover. I had access to a Super Cub on skis—a very maneuverable, high power-to-weight ratio machine that was highly suitable for the job ahead. An observer and I attended a briefing session with the search unit, then we were given a map with our search area marked out in red. I went from the briefing room to the weather office to see what the weather had been over the area on the day the aircraft went missing. The weather had been unsettled, westerly winds and numerous snow showers.

With those weather conditions I thought there would be a good chance the pilot would be on the easterly side of his route. This is because he would likely fly around heavy snow showers and in doing so there is a strong tendency for the craft to move with the wind to the east. While dodging storms, it is hard to keep from drifting with the wind. I have done this very thing over the exact same route! The area we were given to search was of rectangular shape, running north and south, on the easterly side of the pilot's intended route through the Cariboo. Therefore, I thought there was an excellent chance the lost aircraft could be in our search zone and I told the observer to really watch close. "Look for anything unusual," I told him. "One broken tree may be the only visible sign of a plane in the bush."

Our search was over a relatively flat land of forest, lakes and meadows, with only the odd small, family-type ranch. The first leg of our flight was south, close to the western boundary of our area. After flying for some time over bush, we came to a small ranch. I said it would be a good idea to land and ask the people if they had seen, or heard, an airplane on the day it went missing. It was a clear, sunny morning, cold enough to freeze the snow, making perfect conditions for skis. I landed right beside the buildings and a surprised man and woman came out to meet us.

They said they hadn't seen or heard an airplane three days before, but they said they had just made fresh coffee. That was too good to pass up, so we went in the house with them. After our coffee break we had been flying again for about thirty minutes when we came to another ranch. I still thought it was a good idea to talk to the people in this isolated country, so I landed again and taxied almost to the kitchen door.

This time three very surprised people came to meet us—a man, his wife and their grown son. They thought very carefully before stating they had not seen an aircraft on that day, but they did say they had the coffee pot on. I was just about to thank them but say we had better not, when the lady stated, "I just baked a fresh blueberry pie!" Now, there are some things in this world I find hard to pass up, while there are other things I just cannot resist. Fresh-baked wild blueberry pie fits the latter category!

Part way through eating the delicious pie and drinking the fresh brewed coffee, we heard an aircraft. We all went out to look. A thousand feet in the air, flying over us in a northwesterly direction was a Cessna 170. "That's exactly the type airplane we're looking for," I stated. "That's exactly the same kind." They again assured us they had not seen such an aircraft, so we went in to finish our food.

We had been back in the air, searching for about thirty minutes, when a message came over our aviation radio, saying, "Attention all searchers: the missing airplane you are looking for has just flown into Williams Lake." The aircraft we saw flying over the ranch was the missing airplane!

What happened on the original flight was the pilot kept flying around storms, until there was no place left to go, so he landed on a frozen lake with his wheel-equipped airplane. The landing was normal, so they waited through the night. For the next two days the weather was warm, with no chance of a take-off in the soft snow. The third day, with clear, cold weather, they were able to take-off but only after letting some air out of the tires so they would better go over the snow in order to get airborne.

A very happy, if not unique, ending to a search. And, oh yes, the aircraft actually was in the area where I thought there was a very good chance it might be! We would have seen it on the lake if they had not flown out.

CHAPTER 6

Of Wolves

first heard the mournful, spine-chilling howl of the timber wolf in Saskatchewan when I was but seven or eight years old. It was a bitter-cold winter night, when an older brother wakened my siblings and me so we could hear their beautiful chorus. Yes, my spine tingled, even though I was warmly tucked into a bed in the log house on the homestead. We were in the heavily forested, most northerly hinterlands of farmland Saskatchewan. Three miles north of the homestead the arable lands gave way to jack pine ridges and swamps, which continue clear to the pre-Cambrian shield. I have never forgotten the melancholy, piercing song of the wolves we listened to that night on the bleak homestead, so long ago in a world and a life unrecognizable by the young people of today.

After the war we moved to Prince George, B.C., where until the mid-1950s, wolves were very plentiful in northern British Columbia. Roads were few and far between, even in the Prince George area, but drive the twenty-five miles of bush road northwest when snow was on the ground and you would almost surely see wolf tracks. People who lived more than a very few miles from town would regularly hear their howls. To me it is the most thrilling sound that nature is capable of producing, and, yes, my spine still tingles when I hear it.

My brother and I were driving on the old, narrow Chief Lake Road in broad daylight, meeting a vehicle, when a wolf stepped out onto the road right behind the other pick-up. As we got closer, it nonchalantly trotted off into the bush. When the Hart Highway was first built, a pack of wolves jumped from the bush right in front of a car. It was winter so, of course, the car couldn't stop. The driver took a picture of the five wolves he had killed and had a story with the picture in the local paper. The press picked up on this, even those back east, and B.C. was depicted as a great wilderness area full of vicious wild animals, a ruined landscape of endless mountains and high snowbanks on a narrow road not fit to drive over!

Many species of wildlife are very cyclic in nature. A species will rise rapidly if it has an abundant food supply, then if the food supply collapses or gets badly depleted, the species dependant on it also collapses or drops rapidly. Other times, a species will get so overpopulated that a disease will strike it. The self-proclaimed naturalists call this the balance of nature, but in reality it is nothing more than a pendulum that swings first one way then far the other. The most pronounced instance of this is the relationship in the north between rabbits (snowshoe hare) and lynx. When the rabbit cycle is on the upswing the lynx also increase in numbers. They both reach a population high, and then the lynx collapse shortly after the collapse of the rabbit population.

This can be verified by examining the fur-buying records of the Hudson's Bay Co. from their northern posts. From their earliest records, to as long as they have bought fur in the north, the same pattern is seen. There will be a year when relatively few lynx were bought. The next year there will be a few more, then a yearly increase of ever-increasing proportions. The lynx numbers will peak at seven to ten years after their low period. Within a year or two they will crash, again dropping to their low. This corresponds exactly to the seven- to ten-year periods of the rabbit cycles.

In the years prior to the mid-1940s, the wolves of northern B.C. must have had a very abundant food supply. The old-timers said in the 1930s caribou were plentiful in the Summit Lake area, just thirty miles north of Prince George. There was also visible evidence to back this claim. About 1950 I walked through the pine forest, about ten miles north of Summit Lake. Old, shed caribou antlers were actually plentiful. Porcupines, mice, pack rats and other forest folk like to eat shed antlers, but there were still plenty of them left on the ground. This had obviously been an important wintering area for caribou in fairly recent years. I doubt if a single caribou has ever been in that area since 1950.

In 1948, another brother and I drove the long, winding trail from Fort St. James to Manson Creek and Germansen Landing. It was in October and there were about two inches of snow on the ground for the entire distance. A few miles north of Fort St. James we came over a rise on a straight stretch of road, and four or five hundred yards ahead were five wolves. We would have shot at them except for one thing. At that time dog teams were used extensively in the north, thus the wolves could have been some trapper's dogs, at that distance no one could say for sure. As we drove closer, they actually acted like dogs, playing around, paying no particular attention to us. All five were of a predominately gray color pattern and I think we even commented on the fine dog team the trapper had! Then they left. When dogs move, they will walk, run, trot or bound away. When a wolf moves, it goes from zero to full speed in a seemingly effortless blink of an eye. One second they are immobile in front of you, then suddenly, without warning, a blur of movement and they have disappeared before your eyes. When they move like this, you know it is wolves!

Ours was the first vehicle over the road since the light snow had fallen, probably two days previously, and that made for excellent conditions to observe what wildlife had been on the road since the snow. All the way to Manson Creek wolf tracks were periodically on the road. We saw wolves on other occasions, but on the entire road, about 125 miles of wilderness, not even one moose had crossed or walked on the road!

When we asked at Manson Creek about hunting, the first person we talked to told of two men who had come down the Omineca River in a boat and shot two moose. During our time at Manson Creek and Germansen Landing, we heard this story repeated five or six times. The point being that moose were so scarce that the shooting of two was newsworthy. To put it another way, had moose been more plentiful, we would have been told of numerous cases of moose being shot. It was a perfect time to get the winter's supply of meat and to the people living there it was either moose meat or no meat.

The mountains and forests of the Germansen Lake area, as well as west and north for many miles, have long been considered good caribou habitat. They told us at Germansen that Pat Carey, one of the well-known old-time bush pilots, made a hobby of counting caribou. They said Pat told them that in 1947 there was only one herd of fourteen caribou in the entire Germansen area! Caribou are cyclic in nature for some reason that does not seem to be fully understood by the biologists. Wolves may not have been the main reason the caribou numbers were down, but the great abundance of wolves, combined with a dwindling food supply must have been extremely hard on the caribou and moose, both species seemingly at a low ebb.

We returned to Fort St. James a little over a week later. There still had been no other vehicles over the road and no more snow had fallen, but again, much of the road was padded down with wolf tracks. In some places our tracks from going north were completely obliterated by them. Again, we saw wolves but no moose or even moose tracks. When wolves are at normal population levels, many people will spend years in the backwoods without seeing a single wolf!

Wolves are very efficient hunters, and by the standards we set, they are also very cruel killers. It matters not to them whether their prey is alive and suffering beyond imagination while they eat it. One time a bush camp, located about twenty-five miles from Prince George, hired a woman cook. She arrived at the camp in the evening. The next morning she made breakfast, then the men left for the bush. Shortly after they left she heard a terrible scream. She ran outside, looked across the river and saw that a couple of wolves had a deer down. The deer was screaming constantly, a cry that, she said, sounded just like a baby in terrible pain. She went inside but could not stand the cries. She took off, walking, or half running, toward town and went about seven miles on the bush road before she got a ride. She never returned; some very hungry men came back for supper to a cold, bare cookhouse with no cook.

With the obvious abundance of wolves and much evidence of their killing of game animals, great pressure was put on the government to do something about them in the early fifties. Hunting was a major economical and social factor in the province at that time. Nonresident hunters had to hire the services of a guide and the province was laced with guides. The fees from guiding were often the principal income for a great many smaller ranchers, farmers and other outdoors people. The old Cariboo Highway from Clinton to Quesnel, especially, had hundreds of signs listing guides who lived down every road and trail.

In the north, large outfitters used great strings of saddle and packhorses to take well-heeled clients on month-long trips into barely known mountain ranges. If one could see a list of the hunters who went on those long, guided tours, it would look like a who's who of the American, and sometimes world's, elite. Hunters included people like Ken Coleman, the manufacturer of a never-ending list of camping equipment. Many well-known physicians, lawyers and business people made the journeys. A. C. Gilbert, the founder of the company famous for making model trains went every fall for years. Martin Bouvier made annual safaris into the mountains of Alberta that lasted all summer and fall. He took his family with him, including his little daughter, Jackie, who would one day be Mrs. John F. Kennedy, first lady of the United States. Even crooner Bing Crosby went on a month-long guided hunting trip. A nephew of the former Shah of Iran made extended safaris to northern B.C. Edward, the brother of King George VI of England, hunted in Alberta. No doubt about it, these people left great sums of money in the country every year. The province badly needed this heavy boost of annual revenue and was not about to lose much of it because of an overabundance of wolves.

Hunting by residents of B.C. meant not only getting the winter's supply of meat, it was also an important and much looked forward to social event. People from the province's Lower Mainland literally came in hordes, in groups of from two to four or five friends, who then set up tents in some wilderness area in the Cariboo or further north and spent a glorious week or two camping, cooking over a campfire, playing jokes on each other and just having a great time while they hunted. These people, also, didn't want to see wolves taking too much of a toll on the game animals.

Farmers and ranchers throughout the central and northern parts of the province also suffered heavy losses of livestock from wolves. The agricultural society putting heavy pressure on the government was the final straw that ignited the wolf-control program.

The wolf-poisoning campaign that took place in British Columbia in the 1950s has been written about and reported on many times. In more recent years the reporting has all been negative. Most of the articles I have read were written by people who were not there, indeed, some of the critics of the poisoning campaign were not yet born when the wolf program was on and some of these writers had no personal knowledge of wolves! I have a hard time taking seriously anything written or told about the wolf situation by people who have never seen a wolf in the wild or examined their kills. These people rely completely on information they have gleaned from books. One book purported to be factual, by a very well-known author, has now been proven to be fiction! Many "armchair experts" on wolves have quoted extensively from this book. Thus, there have been many myths written about wolves in general and about the 1950s wolf program in British Columbia in particular.

One myth makes it into nearly every article I have read about the wolf-control program. This is the statement that in the 1950s the B.C. Game Department, with the poisoning campaign, was trying to exterminate the wolves! More than a myth, this is a downright lie and, of course, would be impossible to do. When the department decided on the control program, they named registered biologist Al West to head it. Field men were placed in the various regional headquarters. Milt Warren was named for the huge northcentral area, working from a base at Prince George. All field personnel had to report directly to Al West.

The plan was to lower the wolf numbers in areas where they appeared to be abnormally hard on the game. Further, they would try to control them where they were damaging livestock, as well as where the wolves were threatening the very existence of certain pockets of game. For example, mountain goats are not able to stand heavy predation. Thus, it is entirely plausible that goats could be eliminated from some of their mountain ranges. Wolves appear to enjoy mountain goat meat very much. Anyone traveling in mountains frequented by goats will notice that wolf droppings will very often be full of white hair! Therefore, the wolf-control program attempted to protect small bands of goats, caribou and other species of game that were in danger of being wiped out by the efficient predators.

I played a part in the wolf-control campaign. Very early in the program I flew the late Walter Gill, an inspector in charge of the B.C. Game Department for the vast northern division. He had large pieces of frozen meat that had been injected with strychnine. We dropped these baits on the ice on lakes. Strychnine is a very fast-acting poison. When wolves ate the frozen meat, they were always found lying dead seldom more than fifty steps from the bait.

Our task was to not only kill wolves but also make observations about the program. That was why the poison that Walter used was of a fast-acting type. The bait was always dropped well out from shore on the lakes. This was because wolves will travel far out on frozen lakes, but smaller, fur-bearing carnivores do not usually stray far from shore. We were to confirm this by seeing if other smaller species would get at the baits. As a point of interest, it was shown that essentially only wolves got the baits. Out of hundreds of baits dropped, the only smaller animals we found dead were two foxes.

Most of the campaign was carried out in the late winter. In those years the ice seemed to stay on the lakes to a later date than it does now, so many of our baits were put out in April. At this time they would not be covered, at least for long, by snow, but the main reason the baits were put out at this time of year was they would not be out very long until the ice melted, letting them fall into the water and become harmless. Also, this is the time of year when wolves are hardest on moose and other big game as the large creatures are somewhat run down in late winter. Less stamina and poor snow conditions often favor the wolves.

An astute observer can learn much about wildlife in the wilderness by flying at low level over the snow-covered terrain. As pointed out, most of our wolf flying was done in late winter or early spring, when the sun was quite high in the sky. We could distinguish what type of large animal had left tracks, often even in the bush as long as the bush wasn't so dense that we couldn't see the ground. Most of the tracks we saw would be either moose or wolf, and it was easy to distinguish which of these two species had left their sign.

On a smooth, snow-covered surface, a single moose will leave a track that is in many ways very similar to the track of a lone wolf. The actual print in the snow is very near the same size for each animal. The stride, the distance the footprints are apart, is shorter for the wolf, but a small moose would be quite similar, and identification could not be relied upon if stride alone was the only consideration. It cannot be distinguished from the air whether a track was made by a paw with toes or by the split hoof of an ungulate. How, then, could we be so sure of proper identification of the animal that made the tracks? When a moose walks, his left feet make tracks on the left, while his right feet make tracks on his right side. When lined up from in front or behind on a smooth surface like a lake, there is actually two straight lines of tracks. One row of tracks from the left feet and another row made by the feet on the right side, with a space between. A wolf, on the other hand, places each foot in front of the other when it walks. Thus, they leave a track that is essentially a straight line. A coyote's track is not quite so pronounced. This fact, along with the much smaller size, made it easy to distinguish wolf prints from those of coyotes.

Caribou seldom walked on a frozen lake, but we could pick out their tracks in the bush. The way they seldom sank in the snow, their big feet and their walking pattern made it easy to distinguish them from moose or any other animal. The pattern is not quite as wide as the moose and the caribou seem to meander more, giving the impression that they are not sure just where it is they want to go. The animal that makes the strangest and most amusing tracks in the snow is the otter. Otters live in dens, always near a place where there is open water. Their ideal spot is where fast water of a stream exits the outlet of a lake. The fast water will remain ice-free all winter. Otters will use the open water to access the lake, where they go under the ice to chase down and catch fish, their favorite food.

Such a site existed where the McLeod River flowed from War Lake, west of Fort McLeod. Otters like to play, and this was a perfect place for them with the riverbank rising for several feet above the open water. The playful animals would walk around the bank to get on top, then slide down the bank into the water! They must have played this game many hours a day for days on end and year after year, because their slide was worn through the snow and deeply into the dirt. But, one day a very large otter ventured onto the ice, too far from the water for his own safety. The tracks in the snow told the story as plainly as the written word would have.

Four wolves came along. One of them must have been in a bad mood or had indigestion or some other infliction wolves get that render them hard to get along with. Or maybe wolves just behave in a manner that many backwoods people familiar with them say they always act, just killing for fun! The otter was lying dead on the ice. When the animal was skinned, it was proven that a wolf had bit him, but only once. The otter's head was crushed, with the teeth marks showing a single bite by a wolf. The length of the mounted otter rug was an inch over four feet, which is a very large otter.

One time we followed, with a ski-equipped aircraft, the tracks of an otter while it traveled the entire length of a three-mile-long lake. The animal would run for a distance about equal to the length of a house and then slide on its belly. The slide marks were about a third of the length of the running marks. This pattern, jump to get up speed then slide on the belly, was kept up for the entire distance it traveled on the lake!

Walter Gill and I continued with our springtime efforts for about three years. Meanwhile, Milt Warren, the official predator control officer, would be chartering aircraft and dropping large loads of bait, flying from Prince George, Burns Lake and other centers. We did much observing to get a picture of what was taking place. This gave us a great opportunity to see just how wolves operate. The worst possible snow condition for the moose was when deep snow had thawed considerably and then froze. The moose would break through the hard surface, sometimes making their legs bleed from being cut by the icy crust, while the wolves could run on top. Under such conditions the wolves could quickly catch and kill any moose they chose to attack. Even the largest moose didn't stand a chance.

When snow conditions were less ideal for the wolves, they used a different, very efficient method. If they found a moose anywhere near a frozen lake, they would actually herd the animal onto the ice! The lakes commonly had some snow on the ice, but the moose's hooves would go through the snow, then slip on the ice. We often saw evidence of wolves using this technique to get a moose. Tracks would show where the moose had attempted to get around the wolves, to get back in the bush, but the wolf tracks showed where they had cut off any attempt by the moose to outflank them. Once the moose was on the frozen lake it seldom got more than a hundred feet!

When a pack of wolves was finished with a moose, almost nothing was left. From the air a moose kill showed up as a padded-down circle about thirty feet across. Under good sunlight it would show tinges of red, mixed with black, over the entire circle. The black, of course, being what hair was left. Examination from the surface would show the whole padded area littered with small pieces of crushed bone. There are no bones in a moose that a wolf cannot crush!

At the time of the wolf-control program, trappers commonly used dog teams. Of course, we didn't want to kill someone's dogs, so we would contact the trapper if we were on a trap line where dogs were used. One time we saw a trapper on a lake with his dog team, so we landed near him. When he came to the aircraft, Walter Gill told him what we were doing. I had no idea what the trapper's response would be, and when it came, it surprised even me.

When Walter told him we were dropping poison bait for wolves, his face lit up in a show of satisfaction and he said, "Good, I sure hope you get some eagles, too!" He then went on to say that eagles picked off the kits (young beaver) as soon as they emerged in the spring, sometimes getting an entire family of young. Beaver have to cut down green trees, with a preference for white poplar in the fall, then cut them up and skid them into the lake for winter feed. They will commonly go as far as fifty yards, or sometimes they may travel several times that far from the water to cut trees. Beavers cannot move with much speed on land and the trapper told us wolves will wait, then catch the beaver when they are away from the water. Beaver meat to a wolf is equivalent to filet mignon for us!

Later we talked to another trapper on the snow-covered ice of a frozen lake in the wilderness. Again, we heard the same story, eagles and wolves were taking a great toll on the beavers. Also, trappers were now coming in to the B.C. Game Department regional office in Prince George, asking if we could put poison baits on their traplines, too.

The attitude of the trappers toward the wolf program should go a long way in proving that you cannot now judge what should have been done, or not done, half a century earlier. The armchair experts who are so adept at reading books but possess no personal knowledge whatsoever of the conditions existing at the time, should think before they criticize what was done many years earlier. The time of the wolf-control program was many years before this country imported the phrase, "politically correct." It was a time of common sense, if something should be done, just do it. It was a time when people deeply resented excess controls by government, when they were proud to achieve accomplishments on their own and gloried in the freedom that went with it. And no group of people cherished their freedom and independent lifestyle more than did the northern trappers.

Those trappers were hard working and fiercely independent, living in the bush harming no one nor asking for financial help from anyone. The overabundance, as they saw it, of eagles and wolves was causing them undue financial hardship. Other than that, they just wanted to be left alone. Many people do not understand that over periods of time, with greatly different conditions prevailing, the attitudes, priorities and thoughts of people undergo drastic change. No one should try to place a modern judgment on something that happened in a completely different world.

When wolves are just moving from point A to point B when the snow is quite deep, they follow in each other's tracks. Thus, a pack of wolves that have crossed a lake will look, at first glance, as if it was only one animal that made the track. A more careful inspection will determine that many feet have stepped in the same tracks. When wolves are hunting, they spread out.

One afternoon we were flying up a willow-covered valley near the Parsnip River. The valley was covered with wolf tracks, mute evidence that a large number of wolves were hunting. We saw where two moose, one larger than the other, indicating a cow and calf, had previously entered the valley floor from the side. The wolves zeroed in on the tracks with the end of the drama occurring only a mile farther up the valley. The snow was deep, theoretically giving some advantage to the moose, but they didn't stand a chance. The two padded-down circles, tinged red and black, were only a hundred paces apart, in the lonely, pretty valley with its headwaters in the Rocky Mountains.

The wolves were only a short distance away in the willows, sleeping off their great feast, and when our aircraft aroused them we could count them. It turned out to be a pack numbering seventeen animals! A normal wolf pack consists of a family group, usually numbering between six and nine. This group would likely be two family packs hunting together for greater efficiency. The wolves then left the valley, and as they strung out in a line, we could see that their leader was a very large, pure white animal. Of the hundreds of wolves I have seen, this was only the second one that was pure white. Incidentally, the color most often seen was a scruffy black, meaning not pure, shiny black like a Labrador dog, but often having dark brown or gray hair mixed with it. They range from black, through all shades and mixtures of brown and gray coloration to, as pointed out, very rarely pure white.

Some years back a B.C. author wrote a book about a sort of superwolf, pure white, that terrorized central British Columbia. In the book this great wolf led a pack that seemingly could not be shot, trapped or poisoned, as it went about slaughtering ranchers cattle and decimating the wild game population. The B.C. Game Department, as well as some cattleman's association, each placed a large bounty on this particular white wolf states the author in his purportedly factual book. I suppose many people were enthralled as they read about the great strength and cunningness of this spectacular animal. However, one little footnote should be added. The time when all this supposedly happened coincided with the very time that I write of in this article. I had a very close association with personnel of the B.C. game department for several years, covering the time frame of the book and I know that nothing like that happened. There was never a bounty placed on any individual animal. The big white wolf we saw that led a huge pack was an ordinary, large wolf that just happened to be white.

Other times we have followed wolf tracks as the animals climbed a mountain to go after goats. One pack climbed from the valley floor, clear up a wooded mountain always taking the easiest route until they reached alpine. There was a small, remnant band of goats at this spot, which was on the northerly section of Tweedsmuir Park. This band of goats had really taken a beating from the wolves. Had it not been for the interference of man with his deadly poison, I think those goats would have been exterminated. The wolf pack we followed up the mountain, knew exactly where they were going. They had not crossed any other game track and they were traveling together in a nonhunting mode. Mountain goat range usually includes an area of very rugged mountains, where the goats can escape to, but wolves, man or other predators, except eagles, cannot follow them in the steep terrain. However, this particular band of goats were on a range with only moderately rugged mountains for protection, and I think the wolves would have got them all.

Mountain goats always have a home mountain. In good weather they may stray as far as fifteen or even twenty miles or more from it. In this wandering they may easily mix and breed with goats from other home mountains. But there are no better weather forecasters in nature than the Rocky Mountain goat, and at least two days before a storm comes, they will start for their own home mountain in order to be there when the storm hits. Goats winter high in the alpine. In order for them to get food, there must be a slope where the wind will blow the snow off, exposing the grasses, lichen and mosses they feed on. Their home mountain must include such an area, which will be a southwesterly facing slope. Game biologists have told me that if a band of goats is exterminated from their home mountain, the area will remain barren, without other goats moving in to it.

Early in the wolf-control program, the biologist in charge of it gave "doggie bags" to the field personnel in which to collect droppings from wolves. They could then determine what the wolves were feeding on in the various areas. We used to make Milt Warren the butt of jokes, as he would go around with his little baggies collecting evidence for scientific use.

There is one popular myth widely quoted whenever an armchair wolf expert sits down to pen an article on the "facts" about the relationship between wolves and their prey. This cute-sounding myth states that wolves only kill the old, the sick and the weak of the big-game specie they prey on—in short, animals that would soon die anyway.

Dick Turner, who spent a near-lifetime trapping in the Northwest Territories and author of two popular books on the Nahanni country, very strongly disagreed with the premise that wolves kill only the sick and the weak. He once killed moose to feed his dogs, and he told me if he gave the dogs a moose that was thin and in poor condition, there was a change in the dogs. He said they lost weight and energy, couldn't do as much work in a day and in general were just lackluster. Dick also told me that wolves were too smart to eat skinny moose. He said he has seen partly eaten moose, obviously in poor condition when they were killed, that wolves just left and wouldn't finish eating.

Observations made during the extensive campaign of the 1950s showed absolutely no evidence of wolves just killing the sick and the weak. What was seen was wolves killing any moose they wanted to kill. One time we were flying low over a frozen lake, close to shore. There was a fringe of light bush along the lakeshore, then a high, bare, steep hill rose up from the lake. Suddenly, eight wolves sprang from the fringe of bush, running full speed across the ice, heading for the far shore. We wondered what they had been doing in the bush near the lake, so we landed and walked into the trees.

They had killed a moose only a very short time previous. It was a fine young cow, slick shiny black hair and fat, obviously in excellent condition.

As we have pointed out before, wolves are not what we consider to be humane killers. On this cow they had killed, they had eaten maybe fifty pounds of meat from her, every mouthful of which was from the rear haunches. There was not one mark from them forward of the hindquarters! Obviously, death had not come easy for that moose. We followed the trail back to see what the chase had been. The moose had traveled about a quarter of a mile after the wolves drew first blood. The blood increased as she progressed, with the cow going down a time or two before the final onslaught.

Some time into the control program, Al West again gave plastic bags to the field men. This time it was for the purpose of gathering marrow from the bones of moose killed by wolves. From the marrow, they could determine the condition the moose had been in when it was killed. I flew Milt Warren on bait-dropping trips when he was collecting marrow. When we saw a kill, we would land and see if we could get some marrow. On one of those trips we again caught a pack of wolves in the act of eating a freshly killed moose.

This time they were on a lake a short distance from shore and tracks showed they had herded the moose onto the lake, as previously described, and the wolves were reluctant to leave their kill. I flew right beside the moose, with our skis not over four feet above the snow. One saucy wolf had the audacity to actually jump at our aircraft! We landed and had slid along almost to the dead moose before the last wolf left the kill. While Milt was smashing a leg bone to get marrow, the wolves stayed only a short distance away in the bush. They howled as mournful a howl as I have ever heard, I suppose telling all and sundry that a giant bird with a nasty snarl had stolen their moose!

When the wolf program was over, the biologists tabulated the lab results from all the samples of marrow that had been sent to them by the field men. This was very extensive sampling over a wide area of Central and Northern British Columbia. The results of the tests on what condition the moose were in when the wolves killed them did not surprise people familiar with wolves. The tests showed that virtually every moose killed was in fine condition.

A wolf running wild in the bush is a wonderful animal to see.

They are so alert, so keen and so observant. They are very clever in the bush at making themselves invisible to people. Probably a majority of hunters have never seen a wolf in the wild, yet many of them hunt every fall in areas where wolves are relatively common. The casual camper will spend countless weekends at somewhat remote lakes and campsites in the bush without ever seeing a wild wolf, unless it is a wolf that has been feeding on garbage.

These desirable traits the wolf possess that we admire so much, have come about largely because of the actions of generations of people living in the backwoods! Almost every person who lived in wolf country would shoot at every wolf they saw. Let a wolf show himself clear across a wide meadow from a homesteader and, bang, he got shot at. I say shot at, because wolves bring out some trait in people living in the hinterlands that causes them to shoot at a wolf at distances where a hit would be just pure luck. But the miss causes the wolf a great deal of fear. Next time he'll be more careful. Next time he won't stay in the open where he will be seen! The wolf who ventures close enough to people to be shot and killed will not be around to propagate another stupid wolf!

I, too, have shot at wolves from a great distance. And I can attest to their reaction when a bullet whizzes by them! If a moose is shot at and missed, he will likely stay put, probably saying to himself, "What the heck is going on, what was that noise?" Let a bullet fly past a wolf and he explodes, with only a blur being seen as he disappears into the bush. The two wild wolves that I have shot were each hit at such a distance as to cause a knowledgeable person to say the wolves had simply ran out of luck! This reaction to wolves by people living a frontier life has been going on for countless wolf generations, and the wolves have learned.

It is, however, amazing how soon the wolves forget. For example, logging camps long ago disallowed rifles in their bush camps. Shortly after the wolf-control program was over, a pack of wolves found out they could get feed at the garbage dump at a bush camp north of Prince George. And, lo and behold, nothing happened to them while they fed at the dump, which was close to the camp. First they came at night, then in daylight, soon in front of anyone watching them. Once they lost their fear of humans, the people at the camp became concerned. They called the game department and Milt Warren came and destroyed the pack.

One time while the two of us were hunting, we stopped to have our lunch where a trail ended at a river. Soon a wolf was in the river, swimming toward our side. I went for my rifle, but the wolf made it to our side and got into the bush before I could shoot. Ten minutes later the wolf appeared again, casually walking along the trail behind us. This time I shot the wolf, which was not one of the two wild wolves I referred to earlier as having shot. I was really curious as to why he had reappeared, showing no fear whatsoever after knowing we were there. As I walked around, I soon discovered a place in the bush where people were dumping garbage! This had been a garbage dump wolf that had lost its fear of man. It was not a wild wolf, just a ruined garbage dump animal that I exterminated!

A wolf that has lost its fear of people and has no respect for humans is not a nice animal. They slink around, showing none of the fine traits that make a wild wolf so exciting to see—no longer alert, no longer sharp or cunningly clever. Living on the handouts of people completely spoils them. Also, when they lose fear and respect for people, there is a very good chance they may, for the first time in their history, become a physical danger to people. This danger of attack would be especially acute for children.

Anyone who doubts this could happen need only look at what has happened to coyotes that have discovered cities. We watch the news and see coyotes slinking around Vancouver city parks. Already there has been at least one attack on a child. The wild coyotes of old presented no danger, whatsoever, to people. The city coyotes we see on the television look nothing like the alert, sleek and cunning coyotes we see in the wild. The urban coyotes look more like stray, homeless dogs. Let us hope we never see our wonderful wolves behaving like that.

Chapter 7

And Moose

have a special affinity to moose, which began a long time ago. When I was a very small boy living in the hinterlands of northern Saskatchewan during the depression, a strange quirk of nature allowed me to put my hands on a wild moose calf and pet it! A year or two later, when I saw a moose that had been shot, I was astounded by its mass. The head alone seemed almost as big as I was and certainly heavier. I couldn't get over the size of its ears or monstrous nose. After the feet were cut off, I would take one and make tracks in the snow with it marveling at their huge size. As a boy growing up in a largely uninhabited part of Saskatchewan, I became an observer of nature in general and the wild, big game animals in particular.

Elk were the predominate big game in the area, with moose being in no way a rarity but, nevertheless, a bit special. At a very early age I learned to distinguish elk tracks from moose tracks. Elk drag their feet in snow and moose don't. Also, an elk hoofprint is very similar to a small domestic cow with the moose's being longer by comparison. I remember one time seeing two moose tracks in the snows of winter. I stood for fully ten minutes just staring in the direction the tracks went, while my fertile, imaginative young mind worked wonders. I could "see" the two huge animals as they fed in the willows. I could picture the trapper's cabin, the dog team and the whole image of the north the moose tracks represented, before I returned to reality!

Moving to the central part of British Columbia after the war, it soon became obvious that moose were very common and played a major role in the hinterlands of this province. As time went on I had many encounters with the large, black ungulates and will relate a couple of them here. One winter night the late Andy Simonski and I were driving a pick-up truck down a narrow, crooked road. The snow was very deep, and the path so narrow that meeting another vehicle would create big problems. The snow had been plowed with a bulldozer, leaving it piled high on the sides. The snowbanks were, in fact, up to the top of the windows on the side of the truck.

We came around a bend in the trail and there ahead of us was a cow moose with its calf. They trotted ahead a bit as we followed behind. They slowed to a walk for a while, then the cow took a great leap and went over the snowbank and into the bush. The calf stayed on the trail, walking ahead. Then he stopped, turned around and walked toward the truck, with the headlights shining in his eyes. The young moose took on a strange posture as he approached with his head lowered and the hair on the top of his neck standing straight up. He took very short steps, while his feet were in the tip-toe configuration. This was the first time I had seen a moose behave in this manner, and I didn't recognize it for what it was. The moose was in attack mode!

Our truck was a 1950 Chev that had a chromed bumper with a piece of painted metal plate covering the area between the bumper and the grill. The moose walked right to the truck and without hesitation put a front hoof on this metal plate. The front of the truck went down and then he reared right up in the air, bringing his front legs down on the hood. He next beat a rat-a-tat-tat on the hood with his feet, so fast that only a blur could be seen! With that he slid off the hood and stood with his head tilted a bit to the side, with a "What are you going to do about it," look to him.

Oh yes, why have I been calling the moose a "he"? Well, when the moose reared up on the truck, the private parts of the animal's anatomy were less than six feet from our eyes! The animal was a boy moose and a big boy at that. The time was mid-March, so he could have been ten months old. The front feet reached to within ten inches of the windshield, while the perfect imprint of the hoof on the shield behind the bumper was there as long as the truck lasted.

Another time Milt Warren and I were hunting in the mountains. We had shot a goat but couldn't bring the meat back the same day.

So the following day we set out from our camp with pack boards and a lunch to retrieve the meat. To save weight we didn't even take a rifle with us. (See how unconcerned we were about bear attacks in the 1950s?) It was a hard day's work, and in the afternoon it started to snow, which increased the difficulty in getting off the mountain. The result was that it was nearly dark by the time we got down into timber, where we had to immediately prepare to spend the night.

We had to break down dead poplars and drag them to our shelter tree for firewood. A bull moose thought all the commotion surely must be from an amorous cow moose that was just dying for a daddy moose. The bull came charging from the bush directly toward us. Since we didn't want to be the object of his desires, we promptly climbed up the tree we were going to use for our shelter tree! The large spruce tree we had selected to spend the night under had many long, low branches. Fortunately, these attributes also rendered the tree an easy escape route for us to climb above the sex-starved moose.

We were soaking wet. Above timberline it had been snowing substantially, but as we descended first into brush, then bigger timber, the moisture falling was mostly rain. We were also cold, tired and very hungry. The last thing we wanted was to be unable to get by our fire and get warmed and dried out. But every time we tried to sneak down the tree and build up our fire, that lovesick bull would come charging out of the pitch-black bush and chase us back up the tree.

If we were really quiet, we could sneak down the tree and work noiselessly to build up the fire. The method used to get dry around an open fire in the bush is to remove one article of clothing at a time and dry it. For example, one would take off his jacket and hold it close to the fire to dry. When it was quite dry and warm, the shirt would be taken off and the jacket put on. Always the bull moose would be lurking close by and if something cracked or made some other noise, the wacky bull would come, grunting his love call as he came crashing out of the pitch black night. Sometimes we would have to take flight while some of our clothing, even our pants, were being dried by the fire. It was midnight before we finally heard the over-sexed bull walk away through the bush, giving up and finally leaving us alone! Both Milt and I snore with a vigor that may not shake the trees but could certainly be heard for considerable distance through the bush in the quiet of the night in the thin mountain air. The raucous snores would sound far more like a love-starved cow moose than would the noise we had previously made, so it was very fortunate the old rascal didn't come charging back after we were sound asleep!

When the wolf-control program was ending, the B.C. Game Department stationed biologists in Prince George for the first time. Charlie Lyons was the fisheries biologist and Ray Baynes was the game manager. The first winter they were in Prince George, Ray decided to count moose. He chartered the aircraft from the firm I flew for and I took him on the counting ventures. I believe this was the first official, big game counting done in British Columbia by air. Of course, a great deal of flying had previously been carried out by department personnel, but that flying was for the purpose of observation, predator control, law enforcement or patrol. I don't believe any attempt to actually inventory big game, or record numbers or classifications, had been done before. As far as I know, Ray Baynes and I were the first to do this.

We used a Super Cub on skis—an ideal aircraft for the job we were doing. It provided excellent visibility, good maneuverability and lots of power from a very reliable engine. The game manager's plan was not to try and ascertain how many moose there actually were, as that would be an impossibility, rather, he wanted to know how the population compared from year to year. He took maps of the areas, and after a lot of thought and consultation he planned out routes we could fly that would include many wintering areas for moose. The routes were chosen so as to take about three hours of flying to complete each trip.

As stated, we did the flying in the middle of the winter, when the moose were on their wintering grounds. The next winter, at about the same time, we would again fly the same routes so moose numbers could be compared on a year-to-year basis. On the average, we counted just about 100 moose for each hour of flying. One route ended from a southwesterly direction from Prince George, flying down the Chilako (Mud) River. I remember one time counting sixty-six moose on twenty-five miles of this narrow river valley ending at Highway 16, west of Prince George.

Sadly, a great deal of tremendous winter range for moose was flooded when the Peace River Dam was built. Hundreds and hundreds of square miles of choice moose pasture was gone forever. Not only were the people displaced from the valleys of the Rocky Mountain Trench, but also the loss of wildlife was horrendous. Our official moose counting took place prior to the occurrence of this great tragedy. More evidence that the times I write about were, indeed, the glory years in the hinterlands of British Columbia.

Not only did the biologist want to know overall moose numbers, but he also wanted to know the ratio of cows, calves and bulls. The number of calves, in relation to the number of cows, is still a very important segment of game management. For example, in a hunted population of moose, a low calf-to-cow ratio could mean that too many bulls are being shot, thus leaving cows that are not bred. If some of the calves are much smaller than usual, meaning they were born a month or two later, it is a sure sign of not enough bulls compared to cows. Thus, we would, to the best of our ability, classify the animals as to bull, cow or calf.

Since our counting was done in midwinter, many of the bulls had already lost their antlers, which makes it very hard to distinguish a younger bull from a cow. A large bull, even without his antlers, could easily be distinguished from a cow by the shape and size of his massive body. Under very good conditions we could sometimes see the marks on the head where the antlers had been! The biologist was quite happy with the results obtained.

It also became very obvious that Ray Baynes was feeling much more comfortable with the flying, the more times we flew. It was completely natural that he would have an uneasy feeling about the whole thing on the first flight, at least. He had spent several years in university, was newly married, had a good job and now he was laying the whole thing on the line. Here he was in a noisy little airplane with a pilot he had never flown with, going over hundreds of miles of wilderness, often just above the tree tops, trying to see if there were little red marks on the head of a moose!

I had several times seen this same reaction in the foresters I flew. A forester, sometimes fresh out of university or maybe married with a family, would join the company. One of his first jobs might involve being flown into some wilderness area. Maybe the air would be unstable, giving us a good bouncing, while we ducked around heavy rain or snow showers or under low clouds to get to our destination. Maybe that destination would involve landing on a crooked, twisting river. Often these rivers looked too narrow for the wing span of the aircraft until we were almost on the water. Then maybe we would have to turn to miss a big cottonwood tree and get on the short, straight stretch of river in time to stop before coming to a sharp bend. Take-off procedure would sometimes necessitate starting a turn while the floats were but a dozen feet above the water. The foregoing is an exact description of landing and take-off at one spot on the Upper Parsnip River, where we made several trips in and out.

Sometimes the firm would pick out a small lake, maybe little more than an over-sized pond, on an aerial photo and send us to it. I would look at the picture and then tell them I wouldn't guarantee we would land on the lake; I would make that decision after I looked it over. Of course the new forester would be nervous. But there wasn't one of them who wouldn't go right back with me and there wasn't one of them who ever tried to alter my judgment on whether or not we should land in some tricky spot. After a few trips they were all completely at ease and, I believe, enjoying the flights in the bush and the adventures that went with it. Somewhere out there are a lot of pictures those men took of our trips!

Not all of our flying was carried out in adverse conditions. We also did aerial photography of clients logging operations from 10,000 feet above the terrain using wartime Fairchild aerial cameras. For this we required a bright sun with no clouds below us— the best possible flying conditions.

One photography job took us to the west end of Babine Lake. Bob Darnall and I took off the river at Prince George at six in the morning and two hours later were over the site. However, a mile below us was a cloud which prevented photography, so we returned home with no pictures. The next day began with another 6:00 a.m. takeoff, but at 10:00 we were back on the river, again with no pictures! The third flight of this easy, relaxing flying brought the desired results.

To make things worse for the game biologist, the first flight that we took was during a time of extremely cold weather. The morning we were to go, the temperature was colder than thirty degrees below zero Fahrenheit. I was out early and had the engine fully warmed up before Ray arrived at the airport. The engine, with its winter weather protection shields in place, ran beautifully, never missing a beat even in severely cold weather.

In addition to flying in somewhat daunting conditions, there were other problems of moose typing and counting calves. There was always the chance that something, such as heavy predation, may have taken a toll on the calves prior to their being counted. The game manager would have to take this into consideration. Among the things we would be looking for would be wolf sign. Every time we saw where wolves had killed a moose, the biologist would mark the spot on his map. Even with all the variables involved, this was certainly a big improvement in moose management and I am glad to have played a part in its pioneering beginning.

As I stated earlier, one of the two biologists first stationed at Prince George was fisheries officer Charlie Lyons. One time he chartered us to do an inspection of the vast area being logged north of Prince George. One nice stream, a tributary to the Parsnip River, was being badly damaged by the logging. We did a very precise inspection of it, and Charlie made notes and took pictures. He later charged the company involved with damaging fish habitat, based on the information he obtained on our flight. I believe this was another first—the first time a company was charged, and convicted, of damaging fish habitat based upon information obtained by aerial survey. For the last many years all this type of flying, including all game surveys, are carried out with helicopters. But we proved it could also be done in quite a satisfactory way, using fixed-wing aircraft.

There are actually three subspecies of moose in British Columbia. In the Kootenay area of the south is the Yellowstone, sometimes called Shiras, moose. These are an overflow from their main range in Wyoming. They are the smallest of the breed and are considered the least desirable of the moose in B.C. in the quality of their meat. The vast majority of the moose in British Columbia are the midsize Canada, or sometimes called American, moose. Officially, in the very northerly part of the province are the Alaska moose, the largest of the subspecies. Their antlers are different and easily distinguished from the Canada moose. Antlers on the Canada moose spread out, then up, resembling a man with giant mitts on, holding his hands up. The Alaska moose on the other hand typically have antlers that spread predominately outward, then turn up near the ends.

The quality of the meat from moose varies greatly throughout the province. In the south it is very poor, while in the far north it is better than excellent. Old cattle men, my father for one, said the best beef came from an animal that was about three or four and had come through the winter in poor (thin) condition. The beast would then be given all the choice ground grain it could eat. This fattened it quickly and then it was butchered. I think the moose of the north are thinner than their brothers in the south when spring finally arrives. They have no end of fresh green shrubbery to eat and are rolling fat by the beginning of September. The meat from a choice far-northern moose, shot at the right time and properly cared for, is so similar to good beef as to be indistinguishable by most people. Amazingly, the choicest of meat can come from a large bull! But the timing is everything—the large bull must be butchered between mid-August and the first week in September, before the rut starts.

I have stated that officially, the Alaska moose are in the northern portion of the province. But actually, they extend a considerable distance south. They intermingle with the Canada moose and I would think it only reasonable to assume they would interbreed. One day when we were flying on the wolf-control program, Walter Gill suddenly came out loudly with an expletive. "What's the matter," I asked. He said, "Look at the antlers on that moose laying down there, his head is turned sideways over his back, and the one palm reaches all the way to his rear end!" I swung the aircraft around for a better look, and sure enough, that moose had monstrous antlers. By the antlers' shape we concluded the moose, which was in an area west of Prince George, was of the Alaska variety.

One October afternoon Milt Warren and I were in his government Jeep at a small lake about thirty miles southeast of Prince George. As we watched down the lake a moose walked into view, about 400 paces away. It was of monstrous size. Milt Warren and I have each seen more than a few moose in our time, but we were overwhelmed by the size of this one. The antlers were a textbook example of the Alaska variety.

The great bull stood still, carefully looking around. Because moose have very poor eyesight he looked our way without seeing the Jeep in the trees. He then stepped into the shallow lake, put his huge head in the water and ate lily pad roots. He would slowly raise his head, with lily pad leaves hanging from his great antlers, then carefully examine the scene in all directions before putting his head in the water again. We each were using a good set of binoculars to watch him with and were relishing the rare opportunity to observe such a monster moose. Then, upon raising his head he took a little longer inspection of his surroundings, turned and disappeared into the bush from which he had emerged. Moose have extremely good sense of smell, so he likely got a whiff of our scent that had probably drifted across the lake to him.

The event just described is one of those magic moments involving wild game that is permanently engraved in my memory. The whole scene was perfect. The sparkling, clear October afternoon with a definite chill in the air, the distinctive odor of fall, the semi-wilderness lake with no one around except Milt and me and, of course, the main event was the outstanding moose. An artist painting such a scene would probably make the moose a bit smaller so as to be believable!

I have no idea how many moose I have seen in my life, but with just our official moose counting we would see a thousand moose before we had completed the fourth trip. And I couldn't even hazard a guess at how many moose we observed while flying on the wolf program, as well as during my forestry and other flying in the bush. One time I went in to a small lake in August to get something a trapper wanted from his cabin. It was evening and I had to fly low over the shallow lake to chase five moose out of the water to give me room to land!

That scene also became etched in my memory. The low sun of evening highlighting the five moose feeding in the little, shallow lake. The trapper's old cabin with the warm-hue light from the mellowing late sun giving the weather-beaten logs that formed its front a soft, almost artificial, appearance, while large evergreen trees hid the rest of the cabin from view. It was all so serene, almost unreal. It reminded me of a scene a landscape artist might paint in an effort to convince people of just how spectacular the great outdoors really was, and then, like landscape artists so often do, clutter the picture by placing five moose in the little lake! But the noise and presence of our low-flying aircraft soon brought everything into perspective—it wasn't a painter at work after all. The water flying in all directions from the long legs of the big black ungulates as they abandoned their supper of water lily roots to take cover in the bush proved the whole thing really was the work of Mother Nature.

The vast majority of the moose I have seen in my life were viewed from the air but very often from low level where they could be fully evaluated. Disregarding the huge Alaska-type moose I have seen in the Atlin area of the far north, of all the moose I have observed in the northcentral area of the province, only four were really outstandingly large. Three were in the general Prince George area while the fourth was in the Blackwater country farther south. Of course, there could have been outstanding antlers on some of the many bulls we saw in the winter, but they had already shed their antlers by that time. But the very large moose I speak of would have been distinguished by their body shape and size. Other than the one described, watched by Milt and me, the other extra-large ones seen had antlers typical of the Canada subspecies. Whether they had interbred with the larger Alaskan variety or whether they just had great feed and good genes, I have no idea, but they were super size. The bodies were deep and square shaped, giving the impression their legs were shorter than moose legs usually appear.

On Otter Lake, northeast of Prince George, the weathered antlers of a large moose once lay on a sand bar. Without doubt it had once adorned the head of an Alaska moose. Mice and other forest animals had eaten generously from the tips, but a conservative estimate placed the original antlers as having a spread of about six feet. (Most hunters are overjoyed with antlers that are four feet wide—well above average.)

Moose have a very strange history in central B.C., as shown by the following statement. "One of the most spectacular events involving large game mammals in British Columbia has been the southward spread of moose in the last 40 years. Prior to 1920 there were virtually no moose south of the Hazelton-Prince George line." This is a quotation from a B.C. Provincial Museum handbook by Dr. Ian McTaggart Cowan in October, 1965. The time period I am writing about here regarding moose ended in 1962. During that time, of course, there were vast numbers of moose south of the line mentioned. In fact, the records show there was a major die-off of moose in the 1940s in the Chilcotin, after an over-abundance of them.

Ray Baynes transferred to another area in 1960. When he left he told me he had recommended to his replacement that the new biologist have me fly him on his game surveys. But, I never saw the new biologist. He first drove to another town and from another firm chartered the same type of aircraft we were using to do game surveys. They did not return from their first flight and a huge search was mounted. After a few days of intense searching, the now-deceased Merv Hesse found the wreckage. This was at least the second lost aircraft he had found.

Merv's own splendid career ended in a fireball crash on the side of Grouse Mountain in North Vancouver. He, along with Don Jakes, one of the very most experienced helicopter pilots in Canada, was in a large twin-rotor helicopter with six drums of gasoline on board. Part way up the side of the mountain, the helicopter went badly out of control, crashed and burst into fire. The horrendous blaze, fueled by all the extra gas in the six drums, gave no chance for anyone to escape. The official accident report stated a control arm to one rotor blade had come unattached. The two very experienced pilots could do absolutely nothing as the machine flip-flopped into the mountain.

The aircraft Merv found in the snows of the north was a crumpled heap in the semi-alpine, near the top of a low mountain and neither the pilot nor the young biologist had survived the impact of the crash. There were caribou tracks in the midwinter snow near the wreck. The biologist had a camera, and when the partially exposed roll of film in it was developed, it showed the last pictures taken were of caribou in the semi-alpine.

The airplane went in under high power, as indicated by the shape of the twisted propeller. There was no indication of any malfunction of the aircraft. While attempting to get close for pictures, the pilot evidently went into a maneuver from which he could not recover. No one could say with any certainty exactly why the aircraft went into the mountain at rather high speed and under power. One can, however, evaluate some events that could lead to such an uncontrolled crash.

The crash site was not in an area of really rugged terrain, but the treed mountains did rise to above timberline. There are very often quite strong winds at higher altitudes, and those winds can have a profound effect on low-level flying. Remember, an aircraft flies in the air with no relationship, whatsoever, with the ground. This means that if the aircraft is flying with the wind, the speed over the terrain will be the air speed, plus the speed of the wind. If it is flying into the wind, the air speed will be reduced by the amount of the wind speed. Flying crosswind will drift the aircraft sideways. Suppose there is a twenty-mph wind blowing, which is very moderate at higher altitudes and could go largely undetected. An aircraft flying downwind would be going forty mph faster, as compared to it flying into the wind at the same air speed. Think how important that speed would be in the case of an engine failure and the pilot had to land in the trees! Because of the importance of the wind, it behooves a pilot flying at low level, particularly in mountainous country, to be constantly aware of the effects of the wind.

Here is what could have happened to the aircraft in question. The pilot flew past the caribou, below the top of the ridge with the mountain on his left. The pilot then swung to the right for a bit, before starting a 180-degree turn to the left to again come back to the caribou. However, he was not far enough away from the mountain to be able to complete the turn. If there was a wind behind him at this stage, it would literally blow him into the mountain at high speed. The pilot would have the aircraft in a steep bank, trying to complete the turn. The aircraft in question did, in fact, hit the mountain in a one-wing low attitude, indicating it was in a turn and, as we have stated, at high speed.

This scenario, or something very similar, has been the cause of a great many accidents, usually with fatal results. Of all the judgments a pilot has to make that turn out okay, it takes just one wrong call made in a split second to have a fatal ending. There is, however, one thing to be said about making judgments in flying. If at all possible, there should always be a plan B, in case plan A, your judgment call, goes bad. In the example I gave, making a 180-degree turn toward a mountain, there is no plan B. That is, there is no way out; if there is not enough room to complete the turn, the aircraft hits the mountain. And a wind blowing toward the mountain would increase the space required, thus upsetting a judgment based on no wind.

This is why pilots who are familiar with mountain flying and aware of the many nasty tricks nature plays on the uninitiated would never place themselves in such a position. In the situation we are talking about, they would make their turn while heading into clear space, headed away from the mountain. Regardless of the cause, another drama, cold, sad and fateful, unfolded in the hinterlands of the often-unforgiving north. The young biologist had an extremely short career but his name, Hart, was given in his memory to a shooting range a dozen miles west of Prince George.

My name, in a small way, is perpetuated in the official records of provincial history, fortunately, without me having to become a statistic in order that it be there. One of the foresters I flew would sometimes name, and have the name officially gazetted, previously unnamed lakes that we did much flying out of. Thus, northwest of Prince George and just southeast of Great Beaver Lake is Lamb Lake, which they named for me. It's not a spectacularly large body of water, but on most detailed maps it can be found, such as those found in the popular *Backroad Mapbook* series by Russell Mussio.

About forty-five years have elapsed since I flew foresters in and out of it, resulting in it being named for me. I haven't been back to see it since, but maybe I just will go back and see it again. It is about a mile and a half long, a bit kidney-shaped and on quite nice, high ground, as I remember it.

CHAPTER 8

The Old-time Pilots

H ugh Russell came from Prince Albert, Saskatchewan, learning to fly early in the decade of the 1930s. Throughout the years 1937–39, he was bush flying for M & C Airways out of Prince Albert. When the war came, he instructed for the British Commonwealth Air Training Plan in Prince Albert. He was based at the local elementary school, where he was at one time chief instructor, as well as flying twin-engine aircraft at the Observer School.

I have told how the midyears of the century just past was a times when people thoroughly enjoyed life and had a lot of fun. Hugh Russell was a textbook example of this. He could find fun and make a joke out of any situation, and there just weren't enough hours in a day to use up all his exuberance. He credits himself for instigating a fun game they played while the Royal Canadian Air Force students at Prince Albert learned the elements of flying.

At that time in our history the grain from the farmers' crops was harvested by means of a stationary threshing machine. This resulted in straw stacks that stood between fifteen and twenty feet high in nearly every field. In the wintertime, the Tiger Moth training aircraft they used in Prince Albert were equipped with skis. Hughie said one time after a fresh snow, with brilliant sunshine bathing the northern Saskatchewan parklands, the array of snow-covered straw stacks just looked altogether too inviting. So, from the back seat he told the student he had the controls. He then went down and flew over a straw stack, with his skis making a track in the new snow on top of the straw stack! After that he went around and, from right angles, put another track in the snow forming a perfect cross. Of course, a fun game like this caught on quickly, and Hughie said before long there wasn't a straw stack to be found that didn't have ski tracks on it!

Right after the war Hugh Russell returned to bush flying, first in Northern Manitoba and then B.C. About 1952 he was at Prince George, where he was base manager for Pacific Western Airlines. One time I was occupying the right-hand seat of a Beaver with Hughie at the controls; we were on a mail run to the north. I was along as a crew man. After leaving the mail first at Fort McLeod, then Finlay Forks and Fort Graham, we went on to a little lake on Bower Creek and picked up a prospector and his two dogs, then returned to Fort Graham for the night.

The next morning was one of the dullest, most dismal-looking days one could ever imagine. There was a light misty rain and solid, dark, overcast skies with the clouds right down in the trees. If one is familiar with the north, the condition I am explaining will come readily to mind, but very seldom will this weather pattern be seen in the drier southern interior, for example. With breakfast over, we waited around for about two hours, hoping the weather would improve. Then Hughie went to the river and when he came back, announced that he thought we could make it. With Ben Corke telling us to stay, we loaded the mail sacks in the rear of the aircraft, along with the prospector's gear and then the prospector and his dogs climbed in. There were no seats in the rear of the Beaver, so our passenger simply sat on the floor. Passengers sitting on a mail sack was a no-no, but passengers riding in the rear without proper seats or seat belts was commonplace at that time and something virtually all of us did let a passenger sit on anything from soft camping gear and sleeping bags to poisoned, frozen moose meat for wolf bait!

We took off of the Finlay River at Fort Graham into what resembled a tunnel! You could see ahead on the river, but the clouds still hung solidly in the treetops. We proceeded at slow speed and half flaps (foils extended 50 percent, which allows flying at a lower speed and better control. Before we had gone three miles, the cloud ahead seemed to be right down to the water. Hugh pumped the flaps to full on, while assuring me he could land at any spot on the river. We approached the very low cloudbank at slow speed with the nose up into the landing position. Then, with the floats not quite on the water, we could suddenly see ahead. We skimmed under the cloud without getting into one bit of it, and the floats never touched the water! Then we negotiated the turn in the river right ahead of us, while Hugh increased the power, looked at me with a pleasant grin, raised the flaps again to the half position and we continued on our way.

This stretch of river south of Fort Graham had more twists and turns than any other section of the Finlay River. This procedure of slowing down, full flaps, preparing to land, then seeing ahead and continuing to fly was repeated two or three more times before we landed at Finlay Forks. Several times I looked back at the prospector. From his position, sitting crosswise on the floor, the only way he could see out was through a side window. And all he would see through the side window for much of the time would be trees flying past! Every time I looked he was sitting there petting his dogs and each dog was trying to get his attention to receive more petting than the other one. The northerners had terrific confidence in their pilots.

We had dinner with the MacDougalls, fueled up, loaded the mail sacks, then, with Roy MacDougall saying we should stay, took off. We crawled up the Parsnip River, just as we had crawled down the Finlay. After wiggling through an area of low clouds near the mouth of the Pack River, we slid into Fort McLeod. This was the destination for the prospector so he, his dogs and his equipment left us. He seemed happy; I talked with him before he went and not a word was mentioned about the flight at such extremely low altitude.

We picked up the outgoing mail, then made our way up the Crooked River to Summit Lake. But here our trip ended for the day. Hughie flew around the lake, but nowhere did the clouds rise above the trees enough to allow us space to leave the lake. There was a lodge at Summit Lake, so we spent the night there and carried on the next day.

In the high, heavily treed hills east and south of Quesnel is a small, nearly round lake in the bottom of a wooded bowl. Beaver aircraft used to fly in and out of it, but it presented a very marginal condition for taking off. One summer day Hugh Russell flew into the lake with a forester on board. Bud Moore, the engineer, was monitoring the radio at the seaplane base on the Fraser River at South Fort George. Hugh called in, saying he was taking off, then about two minutes later came one of the strangest radio transmissions an aviation radio base operator will ever hear.

Hugh, with complete voice control, stated simply, "I'm in the bush, Bud!"

Bud grabbed the mike and boomed back, "What do you mean, you're in the bush?"

"I'm in an alder patch on the hillside," came the reply.

Later, when Hughie was out, here's how he told it. They had no load, only two of them in the aircraft. It took off, but wasn't climbing fast enough to clear the hills. Hugh put it into a steep turn, attempting to stay in the basin of the lake. In his own words he said, "I had it cranked up as tight as it would go, but I wasn't going to make it. Then I spotted a patch of alders coming up, so I cut the throttle and went into the alder bushes." Not only did they walk away from it, but also neither man had any sign of a scratch or bump! And, of course, the radio still worked. A lesser pilot would have kept trying to clear the ground until he made an uncontrolled crash, probably killing both of them.

It is amazing how two seemingly identical aircraft can perform differently. Bud Moore called the Kamloops base, asking for an aircraft to come and pick up Hugh and his passenger from the lake. At Kamloops was a veteran bush pilot, with a background similar to Hughie Russell's. He came in a Beaver that, for all intents and purposes, was identical to the one that wouldn't climb out of the little lake.

While the two were waiting to be picked up, Hughie took the radio out of the crashed aircraft. The Kamloops Beaver landed, loaded the two passengers and the radio and then took off without incident! This very experienced bush pilot was later killed in the same Beaver when a treacherous wind on high-mountain Lorna Lake, in the southern Chilcotin, turned the aircraft over on landing.

One fine summer day Hugh Russell was going to take a forester out in a Beaver. He taxied out on the river but stayed there a bit longer than usual before take-off. He told his passenger he didn't feel too well and was going back. Before the aircraft got back Hugh was slumped over the controls. He just aimed at shore and the aircraft ran into the dock. He was unconscious when they removed him. Had Hughie taxied out one or two minutes earlier, they would have been airborne when he took ill and an almost certain, likely fatal, crash would have occurred. I imagine the forester in the passenger seat has had a few bad dreams about that episode!

Hughie's wife was a nurse and on duty at the Prince George hospital at the time. She was one of the medical staff alerted that a heart attack victim was coming in, but she had no idea it was Hugh until she saw him! Unfortunately, it was too late for medical help.

Later, his wife told me more about Hugh's early flying activities than Hughie ever did. In the early years in Saskatchewan he flew for a company that sent two or three aircraft to different prairie locations on the weekends for air shows and demonstrations. It was not uncommon for an aircraft to get damaged. She said Hughie and the engineer who accompanied him would patch it up and then, regardless who had damaged the machine, Hughie would say to her, "Come on, we can fly it home!" She said one time another pilot damaged a machine badly. They didn't think they could fix it to fly home, but hours later, after big time work on it, they declared it flyable. Sure enough, she said, big-hearted Hughie said to her, "Come on, we can fly it home!" She was never so scared in all her life. She said hardly a word was spoken until they landed at Prince Albert.

The manager of the outfit lived in Saskatoon, so he flew on home in his own airplane. Mrs. Russell said their phone was ringing when they opened their door. She picked it up and said, "Hello." It was their boss on the line from Saskatoon and he spoke only two words, "Thank God," then hung up!

I think Hughie Russell could fly an airplane better than any other pilot I have ever flown with. And he so patiently answered my questions when I queried him about various aspects of flying and the best way of doing things.

Another old-time pilot at Prince George was Ian Watt. Gray-haired at the time I knew him, he was friendly, outgoing and a top pilot who also liked a joke and a good time. I was amused by the following incident. The owner of sawmill operation, a new private pilot, had purchased a Fairchild 24 aircraft on floats and had flown it without incident. Under good conditions, an aircraft requires less skill to take it off and land it on water, than it does on either wheels or skis. (I have to put in a stipulation here—all of the aircraft I am referring to were of the variety that had a tail wheel. A light aircraft with a tri-cycle undercarriage is extremely simple to take off and land on wheels.)

The owner had attempted to fly the Fairchild on skis but cracked it up on landing, with the aircraft sustaining major damage. The machine was sent away, returning from the shops a virtually new airplane. It sat on the tarmac at the Prince George airport with its first-class paint job glistening beautifully in the sun. The owner called me, asking if I would check him out on wheels. I said I had never flown that type aircraft, so he told me to fly it for a while by myself and then check him out in it.

When I got to the airport, there was Ian Watt. I told him my story and then said to him, "Will you check me out on it?" Ian thought that was a good joke. He laughed, then said, "Go check yourself out."

That particular model of Fairchild, like some of its kin, had a nasty reputation for groundlooping on landing. It had a heavy engine that gave the impression of hanging too far forward. A ground loop occurs when the pilot loses directional control on either take-off or landing, and the aircraft swings violently, then does a 180-degree, or greater, turn on the runway. This usually results in the wing going into the ground and major damage occurring.

This aircraft did not have a steerable tail wheel. A steerable tail wheel is connected to the air rudder by springs; working the air rudder with his or her feet, the pilot is then able to steer it on the runway. With a nonsteerable tail wheel, all steering control on the ground is through the air rudder and brakes. This situation is okay at slow taxi speeds, as well as near flying speed, but as the craft slows after landing, less and less control is available to steer it, thereby greatly increasing the chance of a ground loop. The owner was well aware of this and that was his greatest concern.

So I climbed into the shiny machine, which still smelled of fresh paint and lacquer, and fired up the engine. There was no manual of any sort available, so I just had to figure things out as I progressed. All went well and I considered it a very nice machine to fly. The owner, a large man, was a bit of a nervous type and obviously quite concerned when he got in the left seat, while I was in the right side with dual controls. Aircraft have individual brakes, one on each wheel, with each side controlled by the appropriate foot. This aircraft had brake controls for the pilot on the left side but no controls for the person in the right-hand seat. The individual brakes can be used to assist in steering on the runway. However, since there were no brake controls on the right side of the aircraft that I occupied, I told the owner of the aircraft not to touch the brakes while we were taking off or landing. If he were to overcontrol on the brakes, there would be absolutely nothing I could do to correct it. In spite of his nervousness, compounded by the fact this was the first time in his machine since he had banged it up, we did fine. I flew with him until I thought he was safe enough with it, then let him go by himself. Later he again called upon me for some more dual instruction. After that he flew for a good number of years without damage to any aircraft or himself.

Ian Watt flew out of Prince George for some time, including some of the time Hugh Russell was there. One fall, two years after Hughie Russell put the Beaver in the alder patch, their company Stranraer aircraft landed at Prince George. The "Stranny" was a large twin-engine, flying-boat biplane used for marine patrol off the coast in wartime. Queen Charlotte Airlines once owned this particular one, rating it as an eighteen-passenger aircraft. The large engines were on the upper wing, high above the water. It was a strange, awkward-looking machine, some would say as homely as a mud fence, but it had great capability for getting in and out of small bodies of water. This Stranraer had been in the north all summer, flying drums of gas to caches in remote areas, and was now on the way back to Vancouver.

The Beaver that Hugh Russell landed in the alder patch above the little lake had been taken out by helicopter, but the floats were still at the lake. The pilot of the Stranraer suggested they go to the little lake and grab the floats. So on a dull October afternoon the pilot, his engineer, Ian Watt, another engineer and one more man went to the little lake to bring in the damaged floats from the Beaver. They reported their landing on the lake but nothing more was heard from them, so a plane went out early the next morning to check. The pilot of the search plane found the big Stranraer on the side of the hill, a completely burned-out hulk. It, too, apparently could not climb out of the basin and no one had survived the fiery crash.

That same afternoon I had a tentative flight scheduled with a forester and was to wait by the phone for confirmation. For some unknown reason, I just disappeared for the afternoon—the first time I had ever done such a thing. I simply went off by myself. The next morning I had to make up some excuse for my action because the forester did phone for a flight. Right after that, I heard the news about the crash with my friend Ian Watt on board. That sixth sense of mine was sure trying to tell me something, again!

The tragedy seems all the worse when an old veteran pilot dies with someone else at the controls. Ian, like most, if not all, other bush pilots had his share of close calls, but he always managed to come through them unscathed. One winter day he was flying from Prince George to McBride. There were very low clouds and he was flying just above the ice, following every bend in the Fraser River, which is quite narrow in that area of its upper reaches. He miscalculated his position on the river, and suddenly out of the foggy cloud loomed a railroad bridge!

A few days later he was over the same route in good weather with engineer Bud Moore. He said to Bud, "The other day I flew under that bridge." Bud replied that he was full of some sort of daddy cow material, saying there wasn't room to fly under that bridge. With that, Ian swung the aircraft around and came back low to the bridge. In the snow on the frozen river under the bridge, the tracks from the skis of the Beaver could be plainly seen where they had made contact while going under the bridge!

Another winter day Ian landed at the Prince George Airport with a story to tell. He had been flying low over the Fraser River in a heavy overcast day with low clouds, making his way from the south. Suddenly, in front of him loomed a steel cable! Without authority, or without even notification to anyone, a logging company had stretched a high cable from bank to bank across the Fraser; it hung far above the river with no markings on it! Ian had again dived under the obstruction to save himself.

My heart skipped a few beats over that one, because three days earlier I, too, had been coming up the Fraser River from the south, with engineer Bud Moore, under a similar cloud condition. We were following the frozen Fraser River, keeping just below the clouds. At one point we remarked that if the weather didn't improve, we wouldn't be able to land at the Prince George Airport because we were then at a lower altitude than the airport! However, as we worked our way north the weather slowly improved, and as it did I kept increasing the altitude to stay just below the cloud. We must have gone over the cable. Had the cloud base not slowly risen, we could easily have ended our careers by hitting the hard, unmarked steel cable!

If one makes a study of the history of Canadian bush flying from the very start of northern operations, it will likely become apparent that one pilot stands out as number one. That pilot would be Punch Dickins, who has had volumes written about his exploits. A World War I pilot, he did experimental extreme cold weather flying for the Air Force in the very early twenties, before joining the pioneer firm of Western Canada Airways, later Canadian Airways Limited, in the mid-1920s. He attained many records with that firm for first-time flights, especially to the northern barren lands and the Arctic. Punch Dickins was awarded the McKee Trophy for 1928 in recognition of his success in opening up the far north to air travel and to his overall advancement of bush flying. In that one year alone he flew more than 1,000 hours!

During the big flood in B.C. in 1948 Punch Dickins, while working for the De Havilland company, delivered the very first De Havilland Beaver aircraft to Prince George. It was actually the prototype aircraft with all the testing and test flights for the development of the Beaver aircraft having been carried out on that one machine. The airplane was supposed to be on a demonstration trip, but when the management of Central B.C. Airways saw it, they talked Punch out of it and purchased it immediately! (Central B.C. Airways later became Pacific Western Airlines [PWA].)

Three of us watched the aircraft circling over the flooded Fraser River at Prince George, then my brother Delmar recognized from pictures that we were watching the much-heralded Beaver, so we went to the river to see it, arriving just as it was taxiing to shore. Punch Dickins got out, apologized for being slow at landing and said he hadn't been to Prince George for a long time and had forgotten where they landed, plus the flooded river was running wild with large driftwood.

There was no seaplane dock on the river then, so he pulled into shore just below the CNR bridge, near a Junkers aircraft belonging to Central B.C. Airways and flown by Pat Carey. Clennell Haggerston (Punch) Dickins and Ayliffe (Pat) Carey knew each other well, as both had flown for Canadian Airways. However, Punch was a long-time veteran with that firm and was in a supervisory position when Pat, a second-generation bush pilot, joined the historic company. They talked for a while, then the two aircraft took off for Fort St. James, the main base for CBC Airways. It was well past sunset when they left on the forty-five-minute flight but to those old veterans, landing on Stuart Lake at Fort St. James after float flying had legally ended for the day due to darkness was nothing.

The new aircraft was registered CF-FHB. An engineer looked at the registration, FHB, then said. "Hmm, First Humble Beaver," a moniker that stuck with the machine. The aircraft had a very active life in British Columbia before plying the wilderness skies of northern Saskatchewan. After that it was purchased by the National Aviation Museum in Ottawa, where it resides today.

Incidentally, a Junkers 34 aircraft, one of four or five once operated by Central B.C. Airways, is also in the museum at Ottawa. It may or may not have been the same Junkers that was at the Fraser River when Punch delivered the new Beaver. The museum Junkers was registered CF-ATF, and was purchased new by Canadian Airways of Winnipeg in 1932. The aircraft went to Canadian Pacific Airlines when that company purchased Canadian Airways in 1941. After that it went to Central B.C. Airways (later PWA). It flew until 1960, twenty-eight years, when it was purchased by the National Aviation Museum. Then, in 1962 it made the last flight of any Junkers in Canada, when it was flown from Kamloops to Ottawa. Early in its long career it was often in the Arctic, in both the winter and summer. Some experienced pilots, including Hughie Russell, said they preferred the Junkers 34 to the Beaver.

After having made a study of early bush flying, one would have a short list of maybe three names to choose from to decide the second most-famous pilot behind Punch Dickens. One of those names would be Walter Gilbert, also a World War I pilot, who may have actually flown more accident-free hours than any other early bush pilot. Many of those hours were also flown in the Arctic while Walter was employed by Western Canada Airways (later to become the prestigious Canadian Airways Limited). Western Canada Airways originated the most famous flying insignia in Canadian history, maybe even the world, the flying Canada goose, which was painted on the sides of their aircraft. Canadian Airways slightly altered it, a large circle, blue in the center with a Canada goose in flight and the company name around the outer edge. Canadian Pacific Airlines kept the insignia when they purchased Canadian Airways and the famous goose became known and adored worldwide, from being prominently displayed on all CPA airliners.

Walter Gilbert's autobiography, written with the help of another writer in 1939, is entitled *Arctic Pilot*. In the 1930s he was also flying in and out of Two Brothers Lake in northern B.C., servicing the gold mining operation mentioned in a previous chapter. Walter Gilbert was awarded the McKee Trophy for 1933 in recognition of his pioneering work in advancing aviation in Canada. In 1946, Walter Gilbert and Russ Baker formed Central B.C. Airways that, as stated later developed into Pacific Western Airlines. In the early years of the new airlines existence, Walter flew from the Prince George base and Russ was at Fort St. James. While in Prince George, Walter constantly wired flowers to his wife, back in Winnipeg. His wife, Jeanne, was credited as having ridden more miles in aircraft, prior to World War II, than any other woman in Canada!

Roy MacDougall told me the two founders of the new airline came to Finlay Forks for a few days to build a wharf. Roy and Marge both said they sure liked Walter Gilbert, but they didn't like Russ Baker! And that about sums it up. Walter Gilbert was too nice a person to be co-owner of the cutthroat company the new air service evolved into and he was soon bought out.

Pilot Pat Carey had a checkered career. He most likely crashed more aircraft than any other bush pilot! But, amazingly, no one ever seemed to get hurt in the crashes. One federal government employee who did a lot of flying with the bush airlines said he preferred to fly with Pat, because he said other pilots killed people in crashes but with Pat everyone walked away! Pat was reckless (no pun intended) and many people who had flown with him, or knew him well, had scary stories to tell. Every bush pilot flew low in low cloud conditions because it was the only way they could travel. But, in good weather they would fly from 2,000 to 5,000 feet above the terrain. This allowed for a fair length of time if something went wrong, such as an engine failure, to glide to some area where a reasonable forced landing could be carried out if the problem couldn't be corrected. Pat Carey would sometimes fly the entire route from Fort Ware to Prince George in good weather and never get more than 100 feet above the trees—for no particular reason!

Having an aircraft crash because the machine ran out of fuel is considered one of the worst errors a pilot can commit. A pilot can find an excuse for some crack-ups, but the powers to be will listen to no excuse for running out of fuel. One winter afternoon about

1949, Pat Carey was on a flight from Fort Ware, intending to land at Prince George just before dark. There was an engineer with him, plus a trapper and a load of wild fur in the rear of a Junkers.

About eighteen miles north of Prince George the engine quit. There were nice level, snow-covered fields in the area just north of the Salmon River, but Pat didn't have enough altitude to glide to one. He had the engineer tell the trapper to move to the rear of the aircraft. Weight in the rear of an aircraft will allow for slightly less speed on landing. They were going into a forest of good-sized poplar trees and the trapper had just moved to the rear of the aircraft when they hit the bush.

At this point I will digress to say something about the Junkers airplanes. They were low-wing, all-metal aircraft with heavy corrugated aluminum alloy covering over an exceptionally strong frame. In short, they were built like a proverbial brick outhouse. And there was a good reason for this. The armistice agreement with Germany signed after World War I, included a clause that forbade Germany from manufacturing military type aircraft. So they did the next best thing. They designed and built heavy all-metal transport aircraft in factories that could easily be retooled for military aircraft. After some smaller models, the Junkers W34, with a fifty-eight-and-a-half-foot wingspan came along in 1929. They were made until the mid-1930s, and the ones used in Canada were fitted with the 600-horsepower Pratt and Whitney nine-cylinder radial engine.

A much larger model, the Ju 52, was also made, with only one ever used in Canada. This huge single-engine machine was sixty feet long, with a wingspan of nearly 100 feet. It was the largest aircraft flying in Canada at the time and was aptly nicknamed the flying boxcar. The exact same aircraft, only with three engines, was turned out in vast numbers in Germany. This was a major transport aircraft for them in World War II, and Adolf Hitler even had one for his own personal use.

The Ju 52 in Canada owned by Canadian Airways, was registered CF-ARM. In the aviation museum in Winnipeg is a Junkers Ju 52 with the registration letters CF-ARM painted on it. But it is not the same aircraft that once flew the northern Canadian wilderness skies. On the floor under the wing rests a patched-up, monstrous-sized float, which actually is one of the original floats. The Junkers

Ju 52 in the Winnipeg museum was manufactured as a three-engine model, then many years later it was purchased by the museum and modified to be the same as old CF-ARM, with only one engine, for museum display.

Now, back to Pat Carey about to mow down some poplar trees with a Junkers W34. As pointed out, the Junkers was of low-wing configuration that had drawbacks for a bush machine, but the huge, extrastrong wings on the bottom of the aircraft were great for crashing in the trees. Pat's system, which he had worked out to perfection, was to go into a side-slip prior to crashing. This maneuver used to be commonly employed to lose altitude for a normal landing and was (is) vital in a forced landing to get the aircraft down in exactly the correct place. During a side-slip the left wing is lowered, then to keep the aircraft from turning left, the right rudder is applied; this maneuver can be increased until full rudder is used. The aircraft will actually fly about 10 percent slower in this configuration without stalling than it will in regular flight, as well as safely lose altitude. In a normal landing the aircraft is straightened out before it touches the ground. In a crash, Pat Carey left the aircraft in full side-slip to enable the wing, which was lowered and somewhat ahead, to absorb the blow. When the strong, low wing of Pat's Junkers hit the bush, the aircraft swung violently to the left and a tree cut the tail of the aircraft completely off. The cut-off point was only a couple of feet behind the trapper, who had moved to the rear as told!

When all settled down, no one was even bruised. The trapper said it was quite a shock to see the trees so close behind him and he said he grabbed for anything he could hang onto, to keep from falling out of the gaping hole so close to him, where the tail had been cut off. But he said the load of furs acted just like a cushion for him.

But why did the engine suddenly stop? Well, the three of them got to Prince George later in the evening. Pat phoned his wife, said he had some work to do in town and wouldn't get home until late at night. Then he and the engineer got five gallons of aviation gas in a container and were seen heading north out of town in a car! When the Department of Transport inspectors examined the aircraft they found approximately five gallons of gas in one tank. So it couldn't have ran out of fuel, could it?

But that was one crash too many. The company fired him and the insurance companies would not insure any aircraft he was flying. Nevertheless, he was very soon flying again. This time for a sawmill company that had purchased a Waco biplane. Very shortly into this job he flew over the crashed Junkers to show it to a passenger. Now, are you ready for this? While they were circling over the crashed Junkers, the engine of the Waco quit!!!

This time he had sufficient height to enable him to make a perfect landing in a field with the ski-equipped Waco. Also, there was a legitimate reason why the engine failed, so Pat was back in much better standing. When the chips are down, as with a dead engine, the best insurance is a pilot who can land the aircraft where he wants to or crash land in such a manner that everyone walks away!

Pat Carey went on to fly for commercial companies for many more years. Around 1970, a story appeared in the news media about an aircraft that had crashed into the mountains somewhere near Hazelton or Terrace. The report stated it was a very unusual crash because the machine, a single-engine Otter, had actually jammed into a crack in the mountain. It said the wings were sheared off, but the tail was actually hanging out in space! It took a tricky mountain rescue to remove the lone occupant, the pilot, who they stated was not injured. The pilot, they reported, was an old veteran flier named Pat Carey!

From the early days of the first bush flying, an engineer was nearly always riding with the pilot. They did most of the work keeping the aircraft and engine in good flying condition. The engineers shared all the dangers with the pilot but almost never received any recognition for their effort and certainly never had any glory heaped on them for their work.

In early times in the winter, prior to the invention of the oil-dilution system to facilitate starting as earlier described, it was a major chore to get the engine started. They would drain the oil when flying was completed for the day and cover the engine with their tent-like engine cover. In the morning by starlight and long before day broke, the engineer would light kerosene-burning heating pots and place them under the engine to warm it. While the engine was getting warm he would heat the oil on the stove in the cabin they happened to be staying in. When all was ready, the engineer would put the heated oil in the engine and try to start it. If the engine started, the noise from it would awaken the pilot, who would know it was time to get going! If the engine wouldn't start, the engineer would have to drain the oil and begin the whole procedure all over again. Because this was such dirty work, the engineers became known as the black gang.

Pilots, on the other hand, got all the recognition and often a lot of glory for their work. Some pilots thought getting publicity brought them more flying contracts, thus they strived to have their names and exploits in the newspaper as often as possible. Russ Baker was a firm believer in this theory and he was an expert at getting publicity. I guess it must have been a good theory and history proved Russ Baker was adept at it, because he parleyed a one airplane bush operation into a very major Canadian airline. I remember the stories appearing in the Prince George newspaper with monotonous regularity. Game warden Alf Jank used Baker's air service quite often and I think every trip made a story in the paper! There would be details about how the game department was flown on some patrol by, "veteran bush pilot Russ Baker of Central B.C. Airways," and how they covered so many miles in complete comfort in January, etc.

Nothing illustrates the gap between recognition for the pilot as compared to the engineer better than the following episode. Shortly before construction was started on the Alaska Highway in wartime, the U.S. military was ferrying three B25 bombers to Alaska. They went through Fort Nelson, B.C., but got lost on the way to Watson Lake, Yukon. It was January and they had been flying in clouds, but the sky suddenly broke open for them. What they saw below them was a land of snow-covered willows and other light brush, largely devoid of big trees, fairly level and with some rolling hills. Since they didn't know where they were, they decided to belly land the twin-engine bombers in the brush rather than carry on.

All three planes landed in the snow, fairly close to each other, near the headwaters of the Scatter River, just south of the Yukon border. Because of the three aircraft left there, the area to this day is known as Million-Dollar Valley. Of the twenty-four crew members aboard the aircraft, only two were injured on landing. The pilots reported their intention to force-land and gave what they thought was their location. The problem was, they were more than a hundred miles from where they thought they were. Then another U.S. military plane spotted them, but the location it gave was still fifty miles from where they actually were! Therefore, it took some searching to find the three downed bombers.

Russ Baker finally found them and was able to land in the brush near them with his ski-equipped Junkers. They improved the landing area for him and over the course of a couple of days, he was able to fly all the men, along with their secret bomb sights, out to Watson Lake.

Six years later, when Central B.C.Airways was just starting out, some high government personnel acquaintance in Washington contacted the proper military officials, and the result was Russ Baker was awarded the American Air Medal for his effort in rescuing the downed fliers. I read about it under huge headlines in Prince George and other newspapers, but I don't remember reading one word about Russ being accompanied by an engineer.

Frank Coulter was an old-time engineer, having worked for the old Canadian Airways firm. In the early 1950s, while employed by Central, he also did engineering work and signed the logbook on an aircraft I flew, thus I got to know him quite well. One evening three or four of us were socializing, when Frank told the story of the three downed American bombers. He said he was with Russ in the Junkers every hour the aircraft was in the air searching for and rescuing them. He said as they were searching, he looked out his side and spotted one of the downed bombers, then told Russ, "There's one of them over there, Russ." They were circling over the located aircraft, when Frank looked out his side, then said, "There's another one over there, Russ." As they were circling over it, Frank again was looking around and suddenly said, "There's the other one Russ!" Russ and Frank were able to land in the snow-covered brush nearby and begin the evacuation of the crew. Frank Coulter did not get a medal for his effort in the search and rescue!

Nowadays, there are few who remember these plucky, and often lucky, pioneering engineers and pilots. In studying the history of early bush flying one will soon notice that a great many of the famous pioneers, and their historic aircraft, have at one time or another flown out of Prince George, adding to the wonderful history of the area around the great Rocky Mountain Trench.

CHAPTER 9

Sundry Characters and Events

Tony Zlott lived with his wife Martha in their home on Kerry Lake, one of the smaller bodies of water the Crooked River flows through on its course from Summit Lake to McLeod Lake. However, he spent much of his time at his large trapline on the Upper Parsnip River. His trap line was accessible by riverboat by going down the Crooked River, through McLeod Lake, down the Pack River to the Parsnip, then up that picturesque waterway to his cabin on the upper reaches. This was an easy trip if the water conditions were good, but low water conditions meant many shallows with shifting sandbars, requiring a lot of poling, wading and replacing broken shear pins in the outboard. The major airline operating out of Prince George had so many floats damaged on that waterway that one time they wouldn't let their pilots land on the upper Parsnip River. Winter access to Tony's trapline meant a long, tough snowshoe trip.

Tony's cabin on the Parsnip was in an area commonly frequented by grizzly bears and he hated them with a passion. Grizzly bears will often break into a trapper's cabin while the trapper is away, and when this happens they make a terrible mess of things. They had broken into his cabin more than once, in spite of him doing everything he could think of to keep them out.

The foresters I flew occasionally worked in his area and I have landed them on the river right beside his cabin. We admired the effort he made to keep the bears out, which resulted in his little log house looking like a fortress. It had only one window, and the final touch on barricading the window was to solidly spike a piece of cross-cut saw over the bottom of it. This is the type of saw that for many years, prior to the advent of the power chain saw, was used extensively by loggers in the bush. The saw, with its wicked teeth nearly two inches long, was fastened to the log wall in a manner that allowed the dangerous teeth to protrude up. Any bear trying to squeeze through the window would be severely injured.

Martha Zlott had a trapline at their home on Kerry Lake. This lake had a mud bottom and was infested with reeds all around it. The Crooked River, both above and below the lake, was wide and extremely slow moving. It, too, was a mass of reeds on either side of the open water on it. What I am describing was fantastic habitat for muskrats. Martha concentrated on trapping them, which was probably the only thing that kept the muskrats from reaching such high numbers as to eat themselves out of house and home.

Martha trapped great numbers of muskrats every year, which meant she wasn't overtrapping them because the numbers of them remained high. I forget the exact amount she caught, but it was up to something like 400 or 500 a year. The sale of all those muskrat skins sometimes amounted to more money than Tony made on his large trapline! Martha had a fairly short trapping season working from home, while Tony spent months working hard on his distant trapline. When Tony got together with other trappers they would always tease him about his wife being a better trapper than he was! An American moose hunter would also testify that she was a great guide. A grizzly bear once loomed up in front of them, fifteen feet away, and Martha killed it with one shot while the hunter stood motionless!

Northeast of Prince George and southeast of Tony Zlott's trapline, was a wild area of rugged mountains, dense evergreen forests and smaller, fast-flowing rivers, often with major waterfalls. On the right bank of Herrick Creek, locally known as the north fork of the McGregor River, in the heart of this country, once lived a real mountainman-type trapper in a crude, small, but efficient, cabin. Henry Hobe (pronounced Hoe-bee), like the mountainmen of the old American West who only came to a fur traders' rendezvous once a year, very seldom came to any settlement, even though his trapline was not that far away from civilization. His line was accessible by a fairly easy riverboat trip of only several hours duration. But Henry might only make one trip a year to the "outside." He would sell his catch of fur, then take back enough supplies to last him for the next year.

The entire McGregor River, Herrick Creek and Moose Creek area was famous grizzly bear country. Henry Hobe, too, hated them all, and for years he ran a constant battle with them. Maybe he had reason to hate them. He was once climbing a hill with a heavy pack, when a grizzly bear came running down the same path and ran right over him, sending him and the heavy pack flying! Henry survived it all, in spite of the fact he never had a rifle that could even remotely be considered adequate for safely shooting a grizzly bear.

Then Henry Hobe teamed up with a partner. He and Herb Cooke went together on trapping, but more importantly, Herb convinced Henry that a lot of money could be made by guiding foreign hunters in search of grizzly bears. This was the arrangement they had when I visited their trapping cabin one spring in the late 1950s. Herb told me the hardest part of the arrangement was to convince Henry to leave the bears alone and let the paying hunters help keep the bear population in check. Henry, with a near-lifetime of bad memories of encounters with grizzly bears that he hated beyond reason, was hard-pressed to just turn and give the right of way to bears encountered on the trail. But he did, and the two trappers got along very well together. They were of quite different personalities with Herb being outgoing and talkative, while Henry Hobe was quiet, observant and sincere. Both, however, were honest and good natured.

One time Herb Cooke wanted to explore the possibility of guiding hunters on Ice Mountain, a remote area to the northeast of their trapline, in a very rugged, rough country of big mountains. He said it was too far to walk and cut trail to get there to explore, while packing all his supplies. So Bob Darnall who, as stated, was a forester and a principal in the firm I flew for, had an idea. He told Herb to pack all the supplies he would need in a waterproof, metal container and we would drop it by parachute into some little meadow about halfway in.

We already had experience at doing this type of thing. The foresters, in the course of their inventory work in remote areas, sometimes had to walk through the bush from one little lake to another, and it was beyond their ability to carry enough food with them. We would then drop them food into a prearranged meadow along their travel route. We soon learned what size parachutes were required and how to get the parcels safely onto the ground. We even dropped parcels containing eggs, in the standard cardboard carton a dozen eggs came from the store in, without the eggs breaking! And the men in the bush always found everything we dropped.

The container Herb brought us was a tall, steel drum tightly sealed, which weighed about eighty pounds, complete with the food and other items he had packed in it. A little meadow, one of the few places not solid bush, was picked out on an aerial photo, with Herb keeping one print and us another. We rigged up a home-made parachute for the container and one Sunday afternoon Bob Darnall and I took off with it. We easily found the meadow, then did some test runs to determine the best way to drop our load.

The parachute was rigged with a cord tied to the aircraft that would activate the chute, giving it an instant opening, before the cord broke. Bob had the drum by the open doorway, while I made a low pass over the meadow. The operation went perfect. The chute opened and the heavy steel drum landed nearly dead-center in the tiny meadow. The only problem was that Bob stuck his head out to watch the drop and the rushing air took his prescription glasses and flung them, also, into the grassy meadow below.

Sadly, Herb Cooke never retrieved or even looked for his cache of supplies. Before he got the trip arranged his health began to fail, ending his much-loved life of riverboats, neat cabins with gardens planted by them in the spring, guiding, trapping and enjoying the great outdoor wilderness. Thus, if someone finds, or has found, the steel drum of supplies in what was once a wilderness meadow, the mystery of how it got there will be solved if they read this tale.

I have mentioned both the Upper Parsnip River and the McGregor River area as being well populated with grizzly bears. This should not be taken to mean there were a lot of grizzly in all wilderness locations. I saw a lot of backwoods before I saw my first grizzly bear. I am now in the wilderness only a fraction of what I was at one time, but I have seen more grizzly bear sign in recent years than I did in my early years in B.C. beginning in 1946. Logging has provided many sunny hillsides that come green in the spring, providing excellent spring food for the bears. Also, there is so much more food available for them in a new, growing bush compared to a mature, or overmature, forest before it is logged. And the black bears are also thriving in these new areas of greenery.

There certainly have been more bear attacks on people, both by grizzly and black, in the last twelve years than there were during the dozen years beginning in 1946. The media is quick to echo the save-the-animals people answer of why this is so. In their usual simplicity, these highly vocal professional publicity groups who raise great sums of money for themselves on the pretence of "saving" our backwoods beasts, state there are now more people in bear country, hence more humans get attacked. I consider this to be a completely false assumption.

Starting with the gold discovery years, beginning about 1860, the hinterlands of B.C. were laced with people for nearly the next 100 years. In the 1950s when I talked with the old-timers about prospecting, they always told me that every creek in the entire province had been checked for placer gold, with some creeks having had extensive work done on them. Remember, Ben Corke once told me that in the 1930s there were placer miners on every bar on the Finlay River. Also, it is noteworthy that no new placer gold discoveries of any consequence have occurred in B.C. since the 1930s, indicating that all the creeks had, indeed, been previously prospected. Prospectors searching for hard-rock minerals also scoured the country during those years. I have landed on many wilderness lakes and have seen a fair bit of uninhabited, wild and remote country. But at every location I was ever at, I could soon see evidence of other people having been there in years past. And the men who left their marks didn't usually get to those remote areas by the easy method I used. They probably spent weeks or months in the bush, often sleeping outside with no shelter of any kind to ward off an errant bruin.

A relic of by-gone years is the blazed trail. At one time there was a network of blazed trails in the hinterlands, all marked by trees hewed with an ax by the old-timers, both Native and non, who wanted to find their way back to the same place again. How thick the forest was dictated how close together the blazed trees would be. At the time the trails were marked, the blazes were spaced so the next mark could be seen from the previously blazed tree. Blazing was done by slicing off a piece of bark and a bit of white wood under the bark, with a sharp ax. The white wood exposed would be about three inches long by about two inches wide and there was always a blaze on the other side of the tree. The marks showed the direction to the next blaze, with the next blazed tree always being perpendicular to the preceding blaze on that side of the tree. When following a strange trail one always had to check the blaze on the other side of the tree, to see whether the trail went straight or turned. Quite often where these trails crossed a creek there would be a tin can, upside-down over a stick, so a thirsty traveler could easily get a drink from the stream. Every valley, lake, creek and prospecting area had trails to them that one could follow. This accounts for the phrase so often heard in the north when a person wanted to get to some place he had never been to before. He would simply ask someone in the area, "Where do I pick up the trail to So-and-so Lake?"

As late as the late 1970s, my son Garry and I found our way through several miles of hills, big creeks and forest in the north Omineca by following an old blazed trail. More than forty years had elapsed since the trees were blazed and in green trees the ax marks were two inches deep, due to growth of the green trees after the ax had marked them, and of course they were a deeply weathered gray, rather than the distinctive white they had once been. Also, quite often the blazed tree had fallen down. It is sometimes slow and takes some "bush detective work," to follow such an old trail, but it is a fun and satisfying activity. Just maybe, if one sat down on a log on such an old trail, let his mind wander, then looked ahead with closed eyes, he might see a staunch Norwegian blazing the trail!

It is important to remember that all those old blazed trails followed the easiest route to get to where they were going. This sometimes included a round-about way and was often not the shortest route, but it was always the easiest and most practical way to go. Trying to just go cross-country through the bush to some place would be taking an awful chance of encountering swamps one couldn't cross or an area laced with sharp hills, steep cliffs or some other trick of nature that would make travel extremely difficult or even dangerous. An inexperienced person often wants to give up trying to follow an old trail and just go on their own, but this is a very grave mistake in a wilderness country.

To sum it all up, anyone who thinks people are only now in recent years venturing into bear country, has no knowledge whatsoever of the history of our backwoods and hinterlands. Just think of the great number of men it took to mark all those trails, prospect all those creeks and work on all the hard-rock prospecting sites. Think of all the trappers who were in the bush, then tell me there didn't used to be people in the backwoods bear country! The difference was at that time the bears had a fear of, hence a respect, for people. And if a bear forgot this, that bruin would not be around to propagate any more unintelligent bears. In the 1950s I flew foresters into often very remote country, where they would live in a tent until I picked them up, usually a week later but sometimes longer. The sites I flew them to were always in black bear country and, not uncommonly, good grizzly country, yet they never took with them any type of firearm or any other type of defense against bears. And they never had a single bear incident!

While grizzly bear attacks were rare, attacks on humans by black bears were almost unknown. All the old-timers in the bush thought of black bears as presenting about the same danger to them as would a Jersey cow! The first old prospector I talked to about it told me that grizzly bears will leave people alone. "Just don't get between a mother and her cubs, be very careful not to stumble on to one when it is eating and don't ever go near their food cache." When grizzly bears have a large supply of meat, such as a big game animal, they cache what they can't immediately eat. They cover it with dirt, moss or whatever is handy and then put logs on top of that. It makes an impressive looking sight and a novice may easily go right to it for a closer look or to take pictures. But the grizzly will be lying down nearby carefully watching, and woe to anything that comes near his food cache! I have seen these grizzly food caches just at timberline on a mountain, as well as at low level in heavy bush, but I have no pictures of them!

The prospectors who spent every summer and fall in the northern bush carried a firearm for the purpose of getting food. Since there are far more rabbits, squirrels, ptarmigan and grouse than there are moose and caribou in the bush, they almost invariably carried just a .22-caliber, light, single-shot rifle. The tiny caliber cartridge would be next to useless to fend off an irate grizzly bear, but that was the least of their worries.

When I was flying in bush country I also wanted a light-weight firearm to get food with, in case of being stranded somewhere. I, too, chose a .22-caliber, only I had a good quality revolver instead of a rifle. This, with two boxes of fifty cartridges for it, occupied a small place in the aircraft's emergency supplies or in my pack. And one time I shot four grouse with one cylinder of cartridges. However, there was one occasion when I seriously doubted the wisdom of my choice of such a small firearm.

One morning I flew alone from Finlay Forks into a lake in the northern Omineca, intending to prospect the rest of the day, spend the night at the lake and then carry on. There had once been prospectors working at a mineralized area about one and a half miles from the lake and that was where I intended to look. It was an easy and pleasant walk from the lake, through a parklike forest of quite large trees, but well spaced amid tall grass with very little underbrush. The weather was typical of a beautiful August day in the mid-north, bright sun and a stiff, pleasant breeze directly in my face as I walked. Before long I spotted a green spruce tree that had the marks of grizzly bear claws deeply scratched into it. There is some controversy over why the bears do this, but their mark consists of one long scratch down the tree made with the claws of a front foot with power enough to cause deep gouges to be made in the tree.

The size of this mark indicated it was made by a huge bear. Pitch from the tree had seeped into the scratch marks, indicating the mark was probably two or three months old, so I wasn't worried about the bear being close. The claw marks were so wide that I wanted to have some way of proving the great size of the scratch. Not having anything to measure with, I spread my hand wide with the end of my thumb on the claw mark on one side, but the end of my big finger lacked an inch and a half of reaching the claw mark on the other side. My hand spread is nine and a half inches, so the width of the claw marks, from one side to the other of his foot, made by one swipe of his great paw, was about eleven inches!

I was thrilled at seeing the mark of such a monstrous foot, then I turned to continue my walk through the bush. Within a dozen steps I came to a large, dead log that had recently been rolled over—the work of a bear. And by the size of the log, it must have been a big bear. First glance showed it had been freshly turned over, but as I watched, the grass the log had rolled across was straightening up, right in front of my eyes! The log must have been rolled over only short minutes before I stood looking at it. With the quiet walking and going into a rather strong wind, I could easily have stumbled right onto the bear while it was looking for ants and other bugs in the old log.

I began talking, quite low at first, then gradually getting louder. I said such things as, "I'll bet you're a nice, fine grizzly bear and you wouldn't even think of doing anything bad, would you"? Then I began to sing, and if that wouldn't scare him away, nothing would! I have said a .22 caliber firearm would be next to useless against a charging grizzly, but I immediately took the revolver from my pack and filled the cylinder with long rifle cartridges. It may have been next to useless, but it certainly felt better in my hand than nothing. I suddenly decided I didn't want to go prospecting that day, anyway!

When I think of the great freedom and independence we enjoyed in the fabulous outdoors of times past, I realize this great adventure is being increasingly denied to our present young outdoors people. So much of our back country now, if not flooded or leased to a commercial recreational operator, is marked green on a map, meaning it is now some kind of park or protected area. Some classes of protection close the area to almost everything, while other types of protection allow activities but always under the watchful eye of an often-domineering park ranger. Such a type threatened our son with a fine, because our grandson cut a willow stick to roast a wiener with, by a remote lake where they had often camped but is now a provincial park! Parks may be great for the backpackers who like to travel on government cut and manicured trails, carry their bottled water and then set up their tiny tents at sites the park wardens prepared for them, but parks are awful for those of us who like to control our own destinies, find our own trails and camp where we choose, usually near a supply of clear, cold water.

In the high, rugged and stormy mountains between Fort Ware and Fort Nelson in northeastern B.C. and just south of the Lloyd George Icefield is little Fern Lake, the extreme headwaters of the well-known Muskwa River. In recent years I read how the Parks Department people were so proud of the way they were keeping it a wilderness area. They said wardens regularly flew into the lake and cleaned up the campsites, to enable the next occupants to enjoy a pristine adventure, complete with a supply of wood cut for them! Convenient, yes, but a wilderness experience? No way! A wilderness experience has to be synonymous with independence, and independence can't exist when a government employee tells you where to camp and then cleans up after you!

In September 1955 I studied Fern Lake as we circled over it in a floatplane. I decided it would be large enough to take off from with our aircraft and load, in spite of its high altitude, if it were not for two spruce trees directly blocking the only route for a take-off. So we landed, then immediately cut down the two obstructing trees! However, this was still not enough to save a heavily loaded aircraft in recent years that couldn't clear the low, rocky obstruction at the end of the lake and suffered a very serious crash.

At the time we were there, the only occupant of the area was a very large grizzly bear, who obviously made it his private home base. One morning he appeared in a meadow across the lake, looking nearly the size of a plow horse as he fed on the vegetation. Also, across the lake appeared to be a small flag flying from a pole. My curiosity quickly got the best of me, enticing me to walk around the lake and investigate. It turned out to be the tattered remains of a cowboy's Levi Strauss jeans left there some twenty years previous to mark where twenty pack saddles had been abandoned!

In 1934, the French-born American playboy Charles Bedaux coined the publicity stunt of attempting to take four French-made vehicles resembling trucks, only with half-tracks instead of rear wheels, on a grandiose trek across northern B.C. Starting from the Peace River country, the intended route was via Fern Lake, actually named for Mme. Bedaux. And the mountain pass the lake rested in was later named Bedaux Pass in honor of the ill-fated party that never made it that far. What did get to the lake and beyond, was a contingent of men who were marking a route and cutting trail for the French machines. The total number of horses on the safari was 130, under direction of head packer Bob Beattie. Well-known northern cowboy Tommy Wilde, was in charge of the group that went by Fern Lake. Tommy Wilde once threw a diamond hitch on a packhorse for Milt Warren and me, but that's a another story.

The old pack saddles lay undisturbed on the bench above Fern Lake, exactly as they had been placed by the men working for the

Bedaux party twenty-one years, almost to the day, prior to our viewing them. I carefully examined the old pack saddles, hoping to find some I could use, but the ravages of all those winters and summers along with the nibbling of little forest creatures, left them beyond practical repair. I didn't even think to take one for a souvenir, of the historic Bedaux expedition of the mid 1930s! A close examination of the lakeshore didn't reveal any sign that anyone had camped at the lake after the saddles had been left. The odd bushman going through Bedaux pass may have overnighted there but left no sign.

If a modern fly-in camper comes to the lake with the ready-made campsite and wood supply, he may want to walk around the rock wall at the outlet of the lake and look at the remains of the two stumps and trees. Maybe staring at the rotted wood will send his imagination back to a time when it really was a wilderness area! As a point of interest, the bush aircraft booked for use in case of an emergency by the Bedaux party, said they wouldn't land on Fern Lake but would go on instead to Chesterfield Lake. So, were we the first to ever land an aircraft on Fern Lake? Almost for sure we were, because I don't think any pilot would attempt a take-off from that lake without first removing the two trees that we cut down!

The upper McGregor, Monkman Pass area, is not without its share of history. Prior to the advent of the Hart Highway linking Prince George with Dawson Creek in 1952, there was no land connection between the Prince George-central B.C. area and the Peace River block. There also was no road between Prince George and McBride to the east. Thus, the only land connection between the two geographical areas was the railway from Prince George to Edmonton or a much longer roadway to the Peace River area. Until the Hart Highway, it was a ridiculous route to get from Prince George to Grande Prairie or Dawson Creek. One would take the slow road south to Cache Creek, east to Calgary (summer only around the Big Bend Highway), then north to Edmonton, then a roundabout 400-mile trip to Grande Prairie—about 1,000 miles total!

People from the Peace River block were constantly after the governments of the day to build a connecting road to Prince George via Monkman Pass, a straight-line distance of only 180 miles. To add momentum to their efforts a group of people from Grande

Prairie, Alberta, made an attempt to get an automobile through Monkman pass to the CN Railway, or at least to the Fraser River, east of Prince George.

The Grande Prairie residents started out with an old car of about 1927/28 vintage, said to be a Model T, with the words, "LOUIS STOJAN'S GARAGE, GRANDE PRAIRIE," painted on the door. The car was accompanied by horses, wagons, saws, axes, supplies, a great bundle of ambition and a degree of enthusiasm only capable of being exhibited by optimistic northern pioneers. It was a publicity stunt, designed to bring public attention to the fact that it really wasn't all that far, considering that Monkman Pass was a very direct route and wouldn't add a great deal of mileage to the straight-line distance to Prince George.

The residents set out to prove that if a vehicle could be taken through the pass, it shouldn't be too difficult to make a road and surely the provincial government would then build one. The men cut trail with their hand-powered saws and their axes, pulled the car with horses, forded streams, climbed hills, slogged through swamps and eventually crossed Monkman Pass, going from the Arctic watershed, into the Fraser River drainage system of the Pacific watershed.

But after getting through the pass, they encountered soggier land and heavier forest on the westward side of the Rockies, with the result it was now much tougher to make any progress. By the time they got as far as Henry Hobe's trapping area on Herrick Creek, there wasn't enough left of the now-ruined car to have any-thing to pull! There it was abandoned and the enterprise given up, as the party returned to Grande Prairie.

When I was at Henry Hobe and Herb Cooke's picturesque main cabin, the remains of the car lay on a nearby grassy hillside. Herb and Henry were using the engine from the historic car as an anchor to hold a small dock in the river! As a point of interest, as this is being written nearly sixty-five years after the epic trip with the car, there still is no highway through the very gentle and scenic, Monkman Pass, probably the easiest route to cross the Rocky Mountains in all of B.C.!

With no road from Prince George to McBride until the very late sixties, it meant quite a bit of flying was done between the two points. In the early mid-fifties they scratched out a landing strip on a farm, southeast of McBride. When Ray Williston was Minister of Lands and Forests in the Social Credit government, I flew him to McBride right after they made the landing strip and became only the second aircraft to land on it. I can think of at least three different aircraft that I landed on that little strip at McBride. When we flew there on floats, we landed on the river and tied up close to town.

I can look back on quite a cross-section of people I have had as passengers. Besides the foresters and game department personnel told of earlier, I've flown government foresters and fire wardens, a geologist and one time a RCMP dog man and his dog from Williams Lake to a lake east of Prince George where a search was on for a missing little girl. And when I was instructing, a United States Air Force Serviceman from the nearby U.S. radar base came in to learn to fly. Thus, I can say that I once taught a U.S. Air Force member how to fly!!

Far to the northwest of Prince George is the historic mining country of Manson Creek and Germansen Landing. Placer gold was discovered on the creeks there in the very early 1870s, only ten years after rich gold deposits were found in the famous Barkerville area. Manson, Germansen, Twentymile and other creeks and rivers became well known in the mining fraternity and would have been household words nationally, had it not been for the more famous Barkerville gold camp east of Quesnel. About 1937, a vehicle trail was cut from Fort St. James in the south to Manson Creek and on to Germansen Landing on the Omineca River, a distance of about 130 miles, with a branch trail to Germansen Lake.

It was still pretty much a wilderness country when I first saw it in 1948 and it remained that way, with very little change, until the 1970s. Many old-timers spent most of their life in that fine country, with their very existence now only known because of the markings on their graves in the Manson Creek Cemetery. And there are many unmarked graves!

Mrs. Tate, wife of a Prince George doctor, was a very well-known mining entrepreneur in the area for quite a number of years, beginning in the 1930s. She had camps with cooks, bull cooks and bunkhouses housing a goodly number of workers. She brought in large equipment and in general had prospectors working for her throughout the entire area. I have talked to several prospectors who had worked for Mrs. Tate. In 1948 every person I talked to in Manson Creek, or Germansen, would soon tell of some operation Mrs. Tate was running or where her prospectors were working, and by this time she was winding down her mining operations. The women of our modern world who think they were the first of their gender to get involved in, and in control of, commercial ventures in the business world have certainly never heard of Mrs. Tate!

Carl Hagen was a widely known and highly respected man in the Germansen-Manson Creek area. Directly from Norway as a young man, like so many of the pioneers in our wilderness areas were, he was one of the finest gentleman I have ever known. He owned a little resort on Germansen Lake when I knew him. One time the foresters, whom I flew to various remote areas, were working in the north and we flew from Germansen Lake using Carl's cabins as a base.

Like virtually every old-timer I met in the hinterlands, Carl Hagen treated me in a great manner and we spent some splendid time together. The fish that Carl smoked had a reputation for being exceptionally tasty and sought after. He took me to his smokehouse and explained explicitly how he cured and smoked the relatively few trout his clients caught and kept. I have smoked fish on the odd occasion for much of my life, as I still do, but I doubt if I have ever smoked a batch and didn't think of the efficient but simple smokehouse on the edge of a largely remote, crystal clear, pristine lake and the fine old gentleman with the Norwegian accent tending it.

A year or so before I was staying at his cabins, Carl had made a trip to Norway. He said they were using a boat over there that was particularly efficient and seaworthy. He brought the plans home with him and built one for himself. He took me for a ride on the lake to show me how it performed, and indeed it was as good as it was claimed to be. It was something like a glorified riverboat only had a more rounded bottom, and the outboard was in a well, several feet forward of the rear, or stern if you will, of the boat. It handled rough water on a lake much better than does a riverboat and had good performance with just a small outboard motor. With its great seaworthiness it was ideal for him on fourteen-mile-long Germansen Lake that, like any other lake in the mountains, has a reputation for getting mighty rough in a very short while with little warning.

One time during that period of the year when Mother Nature flips a coin to decide whether to stay with beautiful, bright fall weather or pull the switch that brings forth dull, gloomy and snowy winter, Carl Hagen was in Vanderhoof. The local game warden said he was going to make one more trip to Manson Creek before winter, so Carl could ride home with him. At the same time they left Vanderhoof, Mother Nature's coin came up tails and the big switch was activated that brought on winter with a vengeance. They were in snow almost from the start and the farther north they progressed, the deeper the snow became. The government vehicle the game warden had was just a two-wheel drive, large, heavy station wagon of the type often seen in the 1950s. It continued to make its way through the snow, albeit with difficulty, but it was using a ferocious amount of gas.

Finally, at a point on the road thirty-two miles short of Manson Creek, the big thirsty station wagon ran out of fuel! The game warden was thirty-something in age, healthy and supposedly in good condition and being paid by the government. Carl Hagen was in his sixties, was quite a heavy man, not a man that would normally be picked out from appearance as looking like he would be able to walk a long distance under very adverse conditions and any money he received was from his own endeavor. But the young game warden let Carl start out on foot for Manson Creek and get someone to bring him gas!

I heard the story from several people, but Carl himself also told me about it. He said the snow was more than ankle deep when he left the vehicle, but kept getting deeper as he walked. By the time he reached the old store at Manson Creek, he said the snow was knee-deep. He said he sure wished he would have had his snowshoes. His only other comment was, "I was getting pretty tired." Tired or not, he walked the thirty-two miles in less than ten hours! He told me the exact time, which was nine hours and something like fifty minutes—an incredible but true time to complete such a trip in all that snow for a man close to sixty-five years old.

One fall day another old-time trapper, again of Norwegian descent, and a stranger to me, started to talk about Germansen Lake. I paid very close attention when these people talked to me, because I trusted them and their judgment completely, thus I learned a great deal from them. This fellow's accent was quite pronounced, giving him that melodious rhythm that I so enjoyed (enjoy). I can not hope to transform the musical sound to words, but I will try to emulate his pronunciation as it sounded to my ears.

Shortly into the conversation he said, "Ven you land on Yurmansen Lake in the vinter, you must be very careful. You cannot trust the ice!" This was very vital information he was giving me, so I listened keenly to what the veteran trapper was telling me. "Vone time I vas snowshoeing down the lake and I fell through the ice three times in vone day!" He placed great emphasis on the "three times." Then he went on. "I vas getting so mad I had to go to shore and make a fire and get warm, every time."

"Heavens," I said, "How did you get out with your snowshoes on, making it even harder?"

He replied, "I put my pole across the hole and climbed out."

"Oh, you must have had a pole with you," I stated.

He gave me that very patient and knowing look, then answered, "Ven you snowshoe on Yurmansen Lake in the vinter, you ALWAYS carry a pole!"

My first thoughts on the conversation were that somewhere farther north there would have been some old trapper or prospector, most likely with a musical rhythm to his speech, who could have told me there was a spot with weak ice on a bay on the west end of Two Brothers Lake. If only I could have talked to him before I discovered that fact the hard way!

One time I had an amusing conversation with another Norwegian old-timer. This fellow, who again had come from Norway as a young man and still had his strong, melodious accent, was telling me about seldom ever seeing another person when he was on his trapline. Then he went on, "Vone day I vas snowshoeing on the trail when I saw another man coming on snowshoes. Vee yust started to talk ven the other fellow asked me if I vas from Norvay? I said, ya, I vas from Norvay and he said, 'I am from Norvay, too.'" Then the old trapper, with a serious look on his face, looked at me and said, "I vonder how he knew I vas from Norvay?" That was one of those times when I was real proud of myself for hiding all signs of a grin. I stayed stone-faced and simply said, "Gee, that's sure strange how he would know that!"

One summer night the phone rang in our Prince George house at three o'clock in the morning. On the line was Walter Gill, the game inspector for northern B.C., who told me his father had gone to Germansen Lake with the game warden from Vanderhoof and had suffered a heart attack at the lake. Early dawn had just painted the northeastern sky with delicate hues of pinks and orange, when Walter and I took off from the Fraser River at South Fort George and headed northwest. I knew his father, a fine English gentleman.

The early morning sun in the sparkling clear sky had turned crystal clear Germansen Lake into a landscape painters much sought after jewel. The water was a fourteen-mile-long mirror, quietly lying in a green bowl with a serrated edge of rugged green mountains topped with the bright sun glistening off their snow hats. A painter or photographer's dream, but such conditions can be a nightmare for any floatplane pilot not able to handle the worst glassy water landing conditions nature is capable of producing. It is imperative that nothing short of perfection be used in executing the glassy water landing procedure under such conditions.

When we taxied into the lakeshore cabins, the man who met us at the dock had a somber look on his face, too somber. Mr. Gill's heart attack had been quickly fatal. With some difficulty we loaded the large, stiff body into the rear of the Cessna and flew back to Prince George. The RCMP had an aircraft based at the seaplane dock at South Fort George and I knew the pilot and engineer quite well. The engineer was very surprised when he drove to the dock to go to work in the morning and saw a hearse backed up with people unloading a body from our aircraft!

Germansen Lake is still beautiful, still fairly remote and still home to a very good strain of rainbow trout that grow fat, solid and deep red in the sparkling clear water. It still has the tremendous drop-offs that allow a tall evergreen tree to slide off a steep hillside and continue sliding into the lake, until the roots hit a shelf and stop, while the tree is still nearly straight up, with its top below the surface of the water. And the water is still so gin-clear that one can be over it in a boat and see every little root on the tree far below. If you travel on the ice in winter, you had better carry a pole, because the warm springs here and there below the lake bottom still thaws the ice above them treacherously thin.

But something major is missing from Germansen and other wilderness lakes and from the forests of the northern hinterlands. Something that was once an important and very interesting ingredient of the backwoods. The Carl Hagen and all the fine old trappers and prospectors, many of them with the beautiful sounding accent, are all gone and will never be replaced! The modern visitor will scarcely know they ever existed and tourists will see little, if any, physical evidence of their once-great contribution to the country. The only evidence left of their adventurous life will be in the form of holes in the ground near creeks and crumpled heaps of rotting logs, or soil formed from rotted logs, which once were warm, cozy cabins. Those homes sheltered the very knowledgeable and hardy men with the most admirable traits of human nature that ever existed. But the modern visitor will likely never venture far enough along the treed flats near the fast-flowing, clear streams to even see those last remains of a great people.

CHAPTER 10

Unique Events

So many things have changed in the last half century that maybe the era I write about represented the end of the great age of independence, freedom and ingenuity in Western Canada. If something had to be done, people just figured out a way to do it; they carried out those plans, relatively free of any control by anyone else. A fine example of this was the way aircraft were changed over from skis in the winter to floats in the spring.

Floats should be installed on an aircraft at a location adjacent to a body of water from which it is suitable to take-off. To actually install the floats, the aircraft must be lifted off the ground by being suspended from a hoist, which can be attached to the craft. Prince George had good airport facilities, but no landing area on wheels near the water. When Central B.C. Airways started out, they used to like to fly their aircraft to the airport in the spring to do maintenance work. By the time work was completed the ice had all melted, so they had to figure out some way to get the aircraft near the river. Presto, a plan was arrived at about 1953.

As noted previously, veteran engineer Frank Coulter was the airway's head engineer and I would guess he was the source of the idea. They constructed a lift at their new seaplane base on the Fraser River at South Fort George. All that remained was to get the wheel-equipped airplane to South Fort George! For three years, ending in 1956, I carried out the same procedure as they did, used their hoist and when the floats were installed, Frank Coulter would sign the aircraft's logbook to certify the aircraft as being airworthy on floats. Following is a description of the procedure as we did it.

Just at daybreak on a Sunday morning in the spring, two of us would start out with two vehicles. We would drive to the old airport, which is adjacent to Highway 16 West and now home to a racetrack, part of a golf course, shopping mall and other development. This was the airport that was used prior to the building of the present one during war time. Grant McConache's Yukon Southern Airways used this facility.

We would leave one vehicle at this old airstrip, then drive to the main airport, where our Cessna would be parked with its wheels on. The two of us would get in our airplane and I would fly it to the old airport. The last year we did this, the old airstrip was quite restricted by new construction of the racetrack, but we made it okay. Now comes the true but hard to believe part of the procedure. The passenger would get in the car we had left and slowly lead off, while I taxied the airplane behind him! We would cross Highway 16, then proceed down the paved road toward South Fort George, at least two miles away, down a main public road with just an ordinary car ahead to warn any traffic that may be coming! Eventually, we would be at Hamilton Street at South Fort George where we would turn down, go a couple of more blocks dodging signs and light posts and arrive at the seaplane base and the hoist! (According to recorded history, South Fort George once boasted of having a saloon with the longest bar west of Chicago and north of San Francisco. It's a good thing it wasn't there then, or the Saturday night patrons may have been stumbling out on the streets about the time we arrived with our aircraft.) And what did the police say about all this driving an airplane on the public roads? Who knows? No one ever bothered to tell them!

When Central B.C. Airways purchased the Junkers airplanes from Canadian Pacific, they also inherited a huge amount of spare parts, including an older aircraft that had been taken out of service and used for parts. Such a complete variety of components was possessed that it was decided they could construct another aircraft from just the spares. The problem was they could not just build a new airplane and register it without a tremendous amount of testing and paperwork, making the plan impractical. However, a variation to the plan was soon arrived at that would simplify most of the paperwork required. It was completely legal and involved only minimal red tape to rebuild a wrecked aircraft using the registration and serial number of the wrecked machine on the new aircraft. So they went to the poplar bush near the Salmon River and brought out the pieces of the Junkers that Pat Carey had crash-landed there several years previous to "rebuild." They had retrieved the engine shortly after the crash.

In the spring, a shiny new Junkers 34 on floats emerged from the hangar at the Prince George airport, proudly wearing the freshly painted registration letters of the aircraft that once made an ignominious landing into trees on a cold January afternoon. It also had the nameplate and serial number from the wrecked machine but little else. Now, how to get the new aircraft from the Prince George airport to the river for take-off? No problem coming up with great ideas at that point in history, they simply put a wheeled dolly under the floats, rigged a truck to the front of it and towed the aircraft. All traffic on the highway, the only road, leading south from Prince George had to be halted, while the airplane with the fifty-eight-foot wingspan was hauled a distance of just under five miles to get to the river!

They arrived at the bottom of the hill on the highway without incident, but a flood plain measuring 100 paces across still lay between the Junkers and the river. Pacific Western did not have a vehicle that could pull the Junkers across the flood plain. I had access to a four-wheel-drive Dodge Power Wagon with a winch, so they asked me if I would come to their rescue. A couple of hours later we slid the new Junkers into the Fraser River, and Hughie Russell put it through its paces, with a good workout in the air. In those carefree days of yore, they even made a couple of commercial flights with it before the Department of Transport engineers arrived at Prince George to inspect the Junkers and declare it airworthy!

Another little happening that seemed insignificant and completely unworthy of telling at the time, now seems a bit strange and makes me think, "Did we really do that?" I was flying a couple of foresters out of Fort St. James during a very cold spell one January. When we shut down the engine at night we would drain the oil out of it into a pail. We were staying at the only hotel in the settlement, and when we walked to our living quarters, we took the pail of oil with us and went into the restaurant. I went to the kitchen and told the lady cook that we required hot oil in the morning in order to start our aircraft engine. Everything was wood-fired heat and she said she would set it near the big heating stove. I said it would need to be hotter than that in the morning and she replied, "I will heat it on the stove in the morning."

While we were having breakfast next morning, I peeked into the kitchen and sure enough, there sat our pail of oil on the top of the huge wood cook stove, while the pancakes, bacon, eggs, porridge and coffee cooked on the same range! This routine was carried on for three mornings, until we left. Somehow, I get this feeling that we would not be able to heat our engine oil on the cook stove, along with the breakfast goodies, in the restaurant of a hotel at the present time!

I have stated earlier that during the summer of 1956 I, with another instructor, was teaching a class of about thirty students at Prince George. We were flying two Luscombe aircraft that were really kept "hopping" by the keen students, virtually all of whom later graduated as private pilots. That same summer the Canadian Owners and Pilots Association initiated a membership drive. As an inducement to get members to sign up new members, they had a competition with the first prize being a used Piper J3 aircraft to the member that signed up the most new members. The Piper airplane was being donated, for the publicity and advertising it would generate, by an aircraft sales firm in Vancouver.

I was already a member of the Canadian Owners and Pilots Association and when I read about their competition, the wheels started turning. I went to the Prince George Flying Club with this idea. As a club we would gather all the new members for COPA that we could, send in the list in my name and if we won I would donate the aircraft to the club.

Before long virtually all the students and other members of the flying club became members of the Canadian Owners and Pilots Association. The long list of new members was sent in. Then on October 5, 1956, I received a telegram stating I had won the Piper. It would be ready October 15 and I was told to contact the aircraft sales firm in Vancouver that was donating the aircraft. The sales firm kept delaying me and it wasn't until November 5 that I received a phone call stating the aircraft was ready. Bud Moore, an engineer with Pacific Western Airlines, and I, arrived at Vancouver's Sea Island (now Vancouver International) Airport on November 7, 1956, to take delivery of our newly won flying machine.

We each personally knew the owner of the sales firm, but when we showed up we received a very cool reception. No congratulations, no photos of us receiving our prize—nothing. Finally, I asked where the aircraft was that we had won. We followed him out of the sales office. He looked up and down the two rows of aircraft he had for sale, then pointing to a faded red J3 Cub. He simply stated, "That one." "That one" was a pretty sad-looking, old J3, with the registration CF-JHR, sitting in knee-high grass, with one wing low, due to a very soft tire. I asked him when it had last been flown and he said, "I think it flew in June!" This was the aircraft that he had stated two days earlier was ready for delivery, and it hadn't flown, or probably had not even been looked at, for at least five or six months! The owner of the firm that donated the machine signed the necessary papers and then left, not to be seen by us again.

Bud and I went to work on the dirty, neglected aircraft that should have been clean, completely airworthy and tied down near the sales office full of gas and fresh oil. A major storm was forecast to hit the coast that evening, and I desperately wanted to get away before the bad weather struck because this storm was forecast to be the start of the stormy, winter weather. The nice, clear fall weather we had been enjoying was definitely ending.

I drained the gas, flushed out the tank with new gas, then filled it. I also drained the oil, while Bud gave an excellent inspection to engine and airframe, as the sky darkened and the clouds lowered. Finally, I sat at the controls while Bud pulled the propeller. The engine started right up and ran beautifully, while I warmed it up and checked out the engine controls. I shut the engine down, then looked at the control tower and discovered to my dismay that the rotating beacon on the tower had been turned on, signaling the end of VFR flying at the busiest airport in Western Canada!

Light aircraft are usually flown by visual flight rules, meaning the weather had to be good enough to allow flight under the clouds and ensure the ability to see the ground and have a certain amount of horizontal visibility. The rules stated that weather conditions at departure and landing points must have a ceiling of 1,000 feet or better and a forward visibility of at least two miles in order to carry out the VFR rules. The rotating beacon at an airport is turned on when the weather conditions fall below these VFR standards.

At controlled airports there is provision to operate below these standards at the sole discretion of the control tower operator. So, I phoned the tower, explained the situation and asked for special VFR to leave. The Piper had no radio, no electricity, no lights or even a battery, so it was quite a bit to ask for. The tower operator's response was, "What's your pilot's license number?" When I replied, "Commercial, six-five-five-five," he told me where to taxi to, telling me to wait there and when there was a break in the traffic, which was now flying by instrument rules, he would give me a green light to go. His final words were, "Don't come back!"

Piper J3 Cubs originally had a 65-hp engine and cruised at 73 mph with a tank that held enough gas for only two hours and twenty minutes of flying. The original power plant in this aircraft had been replaced with an 85-hp engine, thus the specs regarding speed and duration were unknown. I soon got the green light to taxi to the end of the runway, then immediately received the green signal for take-off. So, without any check flight to test it, I was off and heading into some of the worst mountains in B.C. for the operation of light aircraft.

To get to Prince George from Vancouver, I usually flew the most often used route that went to Hope, then up the Fraser Canyon to a gas stop at Dog Creek. This is farther than the more direct route of going to Squamish, then basically following the B.C. Rail (Pacific Great Eastern at that time) line to Lillooet. But that route offered almost no place on the entire distance where a safe forced landing on wheels could be carried out. This aircraft, with its extremely limited range, didn't carry enough fuel to make either route! Therefore, I would have to head east from Hope to the southern interior.

The first fifty miles from Vancouver were over the picturesque lower Fraser Valley farmland, so I lined-up on an easterly line to check the compass. After allowing for magnetic variation I was a bit horrified to find that the compass was out by more than forty-five degrees! The compasses in aircraft are designed with adjustments that allow for them to be corrected and set on the ground. This is included with the inspections for airworthiness and this machine would fail a certificate of airworthiness inspection with the compass the way it was. However, the man said don't come back, so I was not about to stop the trip just because my compass, the only navigation device, didn't know its directions! I just made a mental note that when I wanted to go east, I would just deduct forty-five degrees from the normal setting. However, on other headings it could be different. I checked north, took the reading I would need in that direction and carried on. I made a quick stop for gas at Chilliwack, then continued.

At Hope, the Fraser River turns ninety degrees to the west after coming from the north. Our two major railways and the only highway of the day, followed it north. My route would be straight east over the Coast Mountains. These high and very rugged mountains were often called the graveyard of aircraft, due to the many light aircraft that crashed or went missing in the treacherous mountains over the years. Several have never been found. But, I was now completely clear of the storm and had perfect visibility through the spectacular mountains. Just before dusk, and low on gas, I arrived at Princeton. Then came one of those annoyingly embarrassing situations a pilot sometimes finds himself in. I couldn't find the airstrip! I cut the power right down to save fuel as I circled over the area it was supposed to be. It was probably past legal flying time for the day when I finally spotted the little strip and got down, with the engine still running.

The next day I got to the Okanagan Valley, then the storm caught up to me. I had left Vancouver on November 7, but on account of the weather, it was not until November 12 that I landed at Prince George! My fuel stops were at Chilliwack, Princeton, Kelowna, Vernon, Kamloops, Clinton and Williams Lake! And all of this with an aircraft completely devoid of radio or electricity and with a magnetic compass, the only navigational device, that really didn't know its directions. This was "seat-of-the-pants" flying at its best. After leaving Vancouver there were no control towers at any of the airports, including Prince George. Kelowna at that time had only a 1,700-foot grass strip.

A little incident at Clinton goes a long way toward showing just what flying, as well as conditions in general, were like in those halcyon days. Clinton, a small town, had a little-used airstrip about a mile away on a bench above town. When I needed a ride into town from such a place, I would first circle over the town and then land. Invariably, someone would come out to see who you were, then give you a ride. In this case it was two boys on bicycles who came. After asking me if I could ride a bicycle, they offered to double on one and let me ride the other! One boy said, "There's a big hill between here and town." Of course, I knew it was downhill, but I told them I didn't know if I could peddle up hill or not. The boy exclaimed, "No, it's downhill. You'll have to use the brakes," he said, quite concerned, "Or else you'll go too fast!"

Just before we left, Les Kerr, who would later be head of Conair, the largest fire-fighting fleet in Canada, but was then flying a spray plane based at Clinton, came. So, with a genuine thanks to the boys for their sincere thoughtfulness, I went with Les after he fueled my aircraft.

The airplane was officially turned over to the flying club and I checked out most of the pilots on the J3. The only sour note of the whole experience was our reception by the owner of the sales firm that donated the plane. To this day I have no idea what bugged him. The fact the aircraft went to a club should have been a bonus, as so many more people would use and enjoy it.

As stated, the aircraft was not in very good condition. The fabric, which is the covering on the complete machine, was nearly worn out and after only about a year of flying it wouldn't pass inspection. The flying club couldn't afford to get the craft re-covered, so it was put in storage and eventually sold. I am not certain it was worth the effort we put in to get it, but it was something different and we enjoyed it at the time.

CHAPTER 11

The Blackwater River

This book has told of the great country and the fine people who once existed in the Rocky Mountain Trench. It has also talked about the splendid characters that once populated the interesting Germansen area to the northwest, as well as the unique country to the northeast of Prince George. But, it should be known that there was also a vast area that used to be home to some great people southwest of Prince George.

This was the Blackwater River country, usually shown on maps as the West Road River, a large plateau area west of Quesnel. This region has numerous lakes, craggy mountains that stretch up to summer ice and beautiful, rolling alpine extending clear to the river's headwaters in the far-off, high and shear Coast Mountain Range. Steeped in history, laced with intrigue and harboring some tall legends, this vast area is all drained by the Blackwater River. The picturesque waterway roars through a very wicked canyon, several miles long, before entering the Fraser River between Quesnel and Prince George. In the days before river rafting in huge inflatable rafts, no one in their right mind would attempt to descend the gorge with the ordinary canoes or riverboats of the day. I don't know whether the river rafters have conquered this gorge, but I do know I have seen every inch of it from the air and, take my word for it, this is the best way to see it!

In 1866, a grandiose project was started that, if completed, would see a telegraph line run from the United States to Russia and beyond. Insulators with wire strung on them crossed the

Blackwater River country, while clearing and other preparation work stretched much farther north before the whole scheme was abandoned when a Trans-Atlantic cable was completed late the following year. This project, known as the Collins Telegraph Line, was responsible for the name Telegraph Creek being given to a community in northern B.C., because that settlement was on the intended route of the telegraph line and great amounts of wire and other material had already been hauled there.

During the Klondike gold rush in the Yukon the overland telegraph scheme was revived and completed to the Yukon in 1901. This line, known as the Yukon Telegraph Line, followed roughly the same route as the Collins line. In spite of it consisting of a single wire 1,100 miles long through bush and mountains, with service cabins and operators every thirty miles, it provided vital communication to a vast, extremely isolated and sparsely populated news-hungry land until 1936. An important relay station on this line was at the Blackwater River. The site was exactly where the road from Quesnel to Prince George, on the west side of the Fraser River, crossed the Blackwater River. The next relay station north was at Norman Lake, just out of the Blackwater drainage system.

As important and historic as this communication system was, it did not bring much public attention to the Blackwater. It took a man talented in many trades, plus a fellow cowboy from Wyoming, to bring wide-spread fame to the upper Blackwater country. Rich Hobson and Pan Phillips arrived in the wilderness area in late 1934, with stars in their eyes, humungous dreams and a influential ranching friend back home. Pan Phillips is said to have received that moniker due to his earlier cowhand work in the Panhandle area of Texas.

The two traveled by horse back for a year or two, over much of the wilderness area of the huge central and western section of the Blackwater drainage system, looking for a place to build their dream ranch. They finally settled on a large meadow, with meandering streams and nearby lakes for the home ranch, with wealthy friends from New York doing the financing. Soon other locations were added and a major ranching operation was beginning to take shape. But, it didn't reach fame as a ranching operation, as it literally came apart during World War II. The ranch expanded by purchasing other ranches considerable distance from the home ranch.

This increased the costs and the area was only marginal ranch land at best, so poor returns prompted the financiers to withdraw their support, resulting in the end of the big ranch plan. Pan Phillips, however, stayed on at the home ranch, operating a modest but well-known ranching operation until about 1970.

The fame came from the prolific writings of Rich Hobson. His first book, the highly successful *Grass Beyond the Mountains*, brought a plethora of instant fame to the Blackwater country and near celebrity status to the two pioneers. Two or three more books soon followed, adding glory to the country and more fame to the two principal participants, Rich Hobson and Pan Phillips.

I first saw the Blackwater country about 1948. It was just starting to come into its own at that time as a splendid area for the sportsman. The area, somewhat accessible to the wheeled, backwoods-type vehicles of the day, was basically the lower part of the river's drainage area. This consisted of a large pine, spruce, poplar and Douglas fir forest, providing a popular area for moose and deer hunters. The Blackwater River itself later became my very favorite trout fishing stream. Today, this river has special status in the fishing regulations of British Columbia. It requires a special angling license, along with other restrictive regulations, in an attempt to maintain its splendid population of wild trout in a pristine setting.

The Yukon telegraph line had only been closed down for a little over ten years at the time I was first there. Thus, the actual line and insulators were almost completely intact. We used to drive our bush vehicles, actually a four-wheel-drive truck, or sometimes a Jeep, along the old trails that were once used for maintaining the line. Once we were following the line through a burned-over area, when the line itself would, from time to time, get tangled in the wheels of our truck. More than a bit of cursing could be heard as the thick wire was cut and untwisted from under the vehicle.

Insulators, mounted on their nice little hardwood brackets, were on every telegraph pole except, of course, where a fire had been. But we didn't think to take any for souvenirs! The buildings of the relay stations for the line were still intact. Again, we just took a casual glance at them, then carried on. Twenty-five years later, after most of the buildings were gone, treasure hunters would scour the area, digging up the old refuse dump sites in search of old bottles and any other antique or relic items they could find.

After the relic hunters were finished, my now-deceased brother Gordon and I, with our wives, spent hours looking for even one insulator. Finally, Gordon found one, still twisted onto its original bracket, which he gave to us. In 1985, my wife Florence and I walked through the bush to get to the old line in a more remote area. Most of the line poles had fallen down and were covered with moss and leaves. Nearly a half-day of walking the line through the remote bush and examining each pole failed to find a single insulator!

As a point of interest, in the north there were fourteen relay stations between Hazelton and Telegraph Creek. In 1957 a helicopter pilot whom I knew, was flying in that area. He went to the old line cabins and discovered the electrical equipment, including the big brass telegraph keys, were still in the cabins. He hauled out 200 pounds, mostly keys. I doubt if a museum was the recipient of even one of the historic telegraph keys!

In the very early 1950s I began flying aircraft equipped with floats in the summer and skis in the winter for private trips with two or three people. At that time it was a recreational-type operation and one of the first areas I started flying to was the Blackwater country. The central and upper river area had completely different topography than the lower, forested region. Much of the land in the upper areas had been burned over some years previous, leaving nearly open, gently rolling terrain. The river, often in basalt rock, either flows through or runs near many lakes. Eager fishermen flying over the very thinly populated country, looking down at all those beautiful remote lakes, often connected by a river that would later gain fame as a trout stream, could barely control their enthusiasm.

On one of our very first trips to the upper Blackwater, we saw people living on one of the upper lakes, so we landed to talk to them—a Native family, living in the very remote area. The man came to us at the lakeshore and a casual conversation was started, but it was soon evident that he wanted to talk about something. Finally, he told us, in far from perfect English, that they had a daughter in the tuberculosis sanitarium near the coast. He said they had a letter to send to her, but no way to get it out. We said we could take it. A great, friendly smile came over his face as he invited us into their home.

He said something to his wife in their language, and then she, too, got the happiest look on her face that one could ever imagine. The man brought the letter, then sat for a while at the table with the envelope that was not yet addressed. Finally, he said, "I'm not much good at writing in English." My now-deceased brother Ira, who was with me, asked if he could address it. With a very obvious look of relief, the man gave the address required, which was written on another letter, to my brother, and Ira wrote the address on the envelope for him. After that, we asked him about fishing in the area and he gave us great information on where to find good fishing.

In my writing of wilderness areas I keep talking about the moccasin telegraph. It operates the same, regardless what geographical area we are talking about, but I will mention again what an important tool it was here in the upper Blackwater, a very thinly populated area. When people met, they would tell each other everything that had happened, or what they had heard, since they last talked to that person, with each carrier of the news adding his or her own twist to it. Where this was really evident was in regards to strangers they encountered, such as us. When this family would pass on the information about us, they would not only tell what happened but also give their opinion about us. I knew people visiting in the north who were never very popular, just because they made a poor impression on the first people they met in the bush! The people given this information would then pass it on to anyone they encountered. If something considered quite newsworthy came along, it was not uncommon for that person to make a special trip to neighbors to pass it on. Thus, in a surprisingly short period of time, all the people living in an entire sparsely settled land would know all that had happened, anywhere. And strangers to the land became part of the system, whether they realized it or not. In our case, volunteering to address the envelope and take the letter for mailing would likely place us in a good light. How much this helped, I don't know, but we enjoyed an exceptionally good relationship with all the Native people of the upper Blackwater.

One time we had landed on another lake and were fishing in the out flowing river. We saw a Native man walking on a trail some distance away, but when he saw us, he turned and came to us. Many of the Indians I met in that area had a different way about starting a conversation. There was no, "Hello," or any other such greeting.

Instead, their opening statement would be right to the heart of what they wanted to say. In the case of the visitor who just came to us, his first words were, "There's lots of deer in Poplar Hills." Neither of us had ever seen this man before, but he came to us and told of a good place to hunt deer! Poplar Hills was not shown on the map, it was a local Indian designation for a certain area, but I, too, knew where it was. He elaborated a bit on the deer in the area then went on his way! Yes, the moccasin telegraph was a great system.

Often the Natives knew lakes or other landmarks in the area by a name different to what the official name was on a map. One such lake was shown on the map as Kluskoil, but known locally by the name "Chinee," pronounced Chy-nee. We often landed at this lake for access to a good fishing spot on the river. When I was talking to any local person, I always used the Indian name of this lake or any other one that I knew. This went a long way toward making friends. I could see the tension ease on the face of a stranger, when I referred to some place by the name they used. They would then often start to talk in a manner that suggested we were already friends.

Such was the case with a stranger, quite an elderly man, who came to talk to me once at Chinee Lake. With very little preliminary talk, he started to tell a story. Talking with these people meant there was often periods of silence. They would say something and then wait in silence, as if thinking and proper protocol called for similar silence also from the other person. In relating his story I am going to attempt to tell it in the same accent he used. This is not meant to degrade or belittle the man in any way whatsoever. Instead, his tone and use of words greatly added to the joy of the story. And in order for me to tell it like it was and, hopefully, for you to get the most out of it, I must do it this way. Also, to get full benefit from the yarn, one must consider the background.

We were many miles from any settlement and probably not another soul was within a fifteen- or twenty-mile circle. I was a young, eager outdoorsman, thirsting for all the information I could get about this fine land, and here was a gentleman who had spent his entire life in the area about to give me some great information about fishing. He sat on an old, fallen pine tree, bark gone and wood weathered white by many years of sun, moisture and wind. He stared into space for a while, then began. "When I was leetle boy, I used to go fishings with my uncle." Moments later, he continued, "We used to go way high in mountains, my uncle and me and we stay over night at a leetle lake. We catch beeg fish in dat lake," and he placed his hands a good distance apart, to indicate a very big fish, indeed. I could hardly control my enthusiasm, through a period of silence that lasted longer than usual. Then, looking right at me he said, "I sure wished I could remember where dat leetle lake is!"

That was one of the hardest times I've ever had to keep from laughing or even smiling. But I remained stone faced and, thus, saved my integrity. He was dead serious and honestly couldn't remember where the lake was. Had he known, he would have told me the location and where to pick up the trail to it. Yes, the blazed trail system definitely included the Blackwater, and the little lake in question would one time have a marked trail to it.

During the 1940s, and for something like twenty-five more years, Pan Phillips was a very well known rancher, still operating from the original home ranch established by him and Rich Hobson. The ranch was in the upper tributaries of the Blackwater, more or less on the southwesterly portion of that drainage system. The closest post office was Anahim Lake, about thirty-five miles to the southwest, as the raven flies. But, if the raven were to follow the trail, instead of flying in a straight line, the distance to Anahim would be about fifty miles. Much of the trail was only suitable for horses and wagon or sleigh travel.

The main supply center for the Phillips ranch was Quesnel, far to the east, by a very roundabout system of trails. Quesnel was where the Phillips family, once a year, drove their cattle to sell. As in the old west, their trails also included rivers to ford and this was touted as the last long cattle drive in North America. The drive did not consist of great numbers of cattle, since the ranch was basically just a family operation, but it was a long cattle drive and it caught the attention of the print media.

The grand old Canadian farm newspaper, *The Family Herald*, discovered the potential for a good story. They noted that Pan Phillips was the star, or at least the co-star, of the pioneers that founded the ranch in this wild land. They noted the name Pan Phillips was a near household word, due to the great popularity of the book by his partner Rich Hobson.

When the journalists arrived in the Blackwater area they were not disappointed. The country was just as they had hoped it would be—vast, with clear rivers, numerous lakes, mountains and, above all, nearly devoid of people. Pan Phillips, with his big Stetson on his head and astride his well-trained horse, looked exactly like the star of a good western movie. Only Pan was no make-believe cowboy. He was the real thing, from his early cowboy days in the Texas Panhandle to his pioneering in the vast interior of British Columbia, resulting in the home ranch and now the long trail drive. He clearly represented the end of an era, the last of a dying breed. In fact, one could state that Pan Phillips himself was the last of the old-time cowboys and few would dispute it!

Their trail rig was classic, a genuine covered wagon pulled by horses. The whole family, which grew to four children, all went on the trail drive. On one fall drive, written about in a story, they had a baby only six months old, but Mrs. Phillips was still able to do the cooking, including, of course, baking bread, as well as taking care of the family.

The usual time to complete the drive to Quesnel was sixteen days. Much of the trip was over what is known as the grease trail. The name came from the fact that prior to white peoples' arrival, Indians used the trail as a route to the coast. Every fall, bands from the province's interior would go to the ocean to trade their ware for eulachon fish, which are basically all oil and fat. This was their principal supply of grease for the winter, hence the name of the trail. (It was also the trail used by Alexander McKenzie on his trip to the coast near Bella Coola in 1793.) When the Phillips' cattle were sold, the family would buy all the supplies they would need for the next year, load everything into the covered wagon and then drive over the long trail to home.

One time I landed at a Native's home on a lake in the upper Blackwater. I have mentioned how starting a conversation was different with these people. Accordingly, his first words were, "Pan Phillips, he go by here two days ago." I asked him how many cattle Pan had this year and he told me, along with some other details. I would pass this information on to whomever I met next. Thus, this time the moccasin telegraph would travel at the speed of flight!

On the west end of Euchiniko Lake lived a quite elderly Native with the last name of Charleyboy. Unfortunately, I have forgotten his first name. Living with him was a young girl, maybe eight or nine years old at the time I knew him. There was nothing untoward nor too uncommon about this. It was just that for some reason, unknown to me, he was raising the little girl.

These people who spend so much time by themselves want to have a story to tell when someone arrives. Sometimes they have to go back a bit to find a suitable subject. One time I landed at the west end of Euchiniko Lake and Mr. Charleyboy came to talk to me. His very first words were, "A boy, he drown, right there," and he pointed to the mouth of the river, which was deep and slow flowing at that point. Of course I was shocked at this information, and I asked him what had happened. "He fall off an airplane, it was a big airplane." His face showed great concern and now I was really baffled, because I hadn't heard anything about it. I wondered if it was so recent that word hadn't yet got out. So I said, "When did this happen?"

He thought for several seconds, and then answered, "I think it was fifteen years ago!" Again, with difficulty, I was able to keep a stone face and simply answered, "Gee, that's sure too bad."

"Yes," he said, "sure was too bad, he seemed like nice boy, maybe fifteen years old."

One year in late winter, I found out we had a couple of flights to make to a lake deep in the Coast Range Mountains to the southwest, the next summer. We would require some extra gas for the aircraft somewhere along the route, so I decided to fly a drum of gas to Euchiniko Lake. It was much easier to get the heavy, awkward, forty-five-gallon drum of gas into and out of the aircraft when it was on skis rather than when it was on floats. So I opted to fly the gas to the lake before the ice melted.

It happened to be Easter Sunday when I was going, so I bought an Easter basket of candies and things to take to the little girl. When I landed I taxied in the snow as close to the lake shore as I could, to make it easier to get the gas drum onto the land. Both Mr. Charleyboy and the girl came to the aircraft. I handed the Easter basket to the little girl, but she wouldn't take it until he said it was for her. She had the sweetest, most genuine smile on her cute little face that any young girl could possibly have. She just couldn't believe it. Very carefully she set the basket down, then ever so gently lifted the little stick-legged chicken from the top of the basket. She carried it in her two little cupped hands to the cabin and then,

I guess, played with it because it was some time before she came back for the basket of candies.

The next summer when we came to the lake on floats, Mr. Charleyboy could hardly wait until the aircraft was on shore to say something to us. I suspected something was wrong. As soon as I stepped out of the airplane, he started talking, almost incoherently. "He stole it—I couldn't stop him. He took it—he took it—" The poor man was in a dither.

When he finally settled down and told us the story, it turned out another aircraft had come and, despite the best efforts of Mr. Charleyboy, had taken part of our gas. He felt really bad that this had happened and I felt bad because of the way he felt, like he had let us down. I tried to assure him it was okay, that it wasn't his fault. Actually, the theft was worse than just the loss of some gas. Aviation gas comes in sealed drums, and once it is opened, the remainder deteriorates. Many pilots are very reluctant to use gas from a drum that has been opened before.

To steal gas from a cache was completely unthinkable. One thing was certain; a bush pilot didn't do it. It was not at all uncommon for a bush pilot to use someone else's gas cache if he had to, but he would always report it and he would arrange to pay for it or replace the gas as soon as possible. This fellow made no effort to replace the gas nor any attempt to find the owner of the gas and report what he had done or leave identification. Knowingly, that is. But from Mr. Charleyboy's description, we concluded the aircraft was a Seabee. This is an amphibious aircraft that floats on the water on its hull, like a boat. We were also shown where the pilot had hit a rock when he was getting to shore.

Walter Gill, game inspector with the B.C. Game Department, was with us. We could see paint on the rock that was hit and Walter, now deceased, scraped off the paint and saved it. Some fairly easy detective work soon matched the paint to a Seabee aircraft with a dent in the front, left side of the hull—and some paint missing!

One would be hard pressed to find a better example of how not to get along in a wilderness country than this. Steal from someone's cache, then get the local people mad at you! By the way, I wonder if that may have been the same Seabee aircraft that later caused me to make a search trip to Fort St. James, when the pilot knew he was causing a false alarm!

After I had advanced my flying skills and qualifications by earning a commercial license, I could get paid for my efforts. One morning a man came to the firm I was flying for and asked for a charter. He further stated he wanted to fly over the Blackwater country to look for ranch land. I didn't encourage him since I knew, of course, the time was long, long gone when you could simply "find" ranch land. However, I was not about to turn down a chance to be paid for flying to one of my favorite areas, so we went.

He said he wanted to see the country anyway, so I gave him a good tour, and then I suggested that if he wanted to know about ranches in the area, he should talk to Pan Phillips. He thought that was a fine idea, so I headed for the home ranch. When one is flying on floats in the summer or skis in the winter, it is common practice to fly to some destination then look for a landing site after you arrive. I had never landed at the ranch before, so I had to look for a waterway to come in on, as close to the ranch buildings as possible. There were a couple of suitable lakes, but they were about four miles away. The only body of water close was a small lake only about a half mile north of the ranch buildings. When I looked the lake over I discovered it was shallow. Very shallow.

The lake was crystal clear and there was a slight wind ripple on the water, resulting in ideal conditions. I flew over the lake about twenty feet above the water, staring down at an angle. I could see every pebble on the bottom of the lake. I judged there wasn't a spot deeper than about three feet in the entire lake! I took another similar pass over it, looking for any shallows or rocks. I could see neither and was amazed to see such an even depth, overall, of the small lake. I concluded it was about an even three feet deep throughout the entire little lake.

When an aircraft is going fast on the water, as when near take-off speed, it virtually skims along on top. This is known as running on the step. But when landing it slows down, then "falls off" the step. At this time the tail end of the floats go down in the water. The same thing happens on take-off, before it gets on the step. In each condition, with the aircraft I had, the heel of the floats would go down maybe two and a half feet below the surface.

It was a judgment call for sure. But with this type of flying, often referred to as bush flying, the pilot is completely on his own, constantly making the judgment calls with no control tower operator telling him what the conditions are, what to do or where to land. This type of flying gave the pilot the tremendous freedom and great independence that was so cherished, but it was also the reason it was not for everyone. I made a routine landing on the little shallow lake near the ranch, but once on the water I realized I hadn't looked for a walking trail from the lake to the ranch. The shore closest to the ranch was thick with alders and a bit swampy. I said there must be a trail from the ranch to the lake, so we took off again to look for it. We saw a fence to the lake further along, so we landed again and taxied to that spot. Walking along the fence soon brought us to a trail.

Soon the trail crossed a creek and by the creek was a young man, bending over, chopping something with an axe. While still a respectable distance away from him, I hollered, "Hello." The very surprised young man was Ken, the oldest of the Phillips family, a very well built, sun browned strapping young man. He quickly recovered from the shock of having two strangers walk up on him, then began a very interesting conversation. He invited us to the house, and as we walked, told us that he was fifteen and a half years old. The Anahim stampede was a big event in the western Chilcotin and since there were only local contestants, it was very popular with the ranchers. That year's stampede was just days away and the Phillips were preparing to go to it. I asked Ken if he competed in the stampede. "No," he said, "I used to when I was young, but I don't anymore!"

Mrs. Phillips heartily invited us into the house and then asked, "Did you see Pan?" When we said we hadn't, she told us that he had gone to the lake on horse back to meet us. She started to make dinner, but had to hold off completing it, waiting for Pan to return. Probably about an hour after we got to the buildings, Pan came walking in. What happened was that the trail to the lake, which we hadn't seen, came from a pine ridge on the east end, while we had left from the south, the side of the lake nearest the buildings. Pan had ridden his horse to the ridge above the lake, then left him to walk around the lake to where we were. When we took off to look for the trail we scared his horse, which took off through the bush with its saddle on and Pan couldn't find him.

I felt awful, but Pan said it was okay and the horse would come back. Mrs. Phillips cooked a delicious meal and two extra plates appeared to make no difference to her. During our after-dinner conversation, I said to Pan, "It must be pretty tricky landing in that shallow lake later in the fall, when the water gets lower." He gave his hearty laugh, then said, "I wouldn't know, you're the first pilot who ever landed on it!" A bit shocked, I asked where they landed and he said, "If you come again, fly over the ranch, then land at Tsilbekuz Lake and I will get you with the team and wagon."

"But that's four miles away," I protested, "That's too far to go with the horses."

"No, no that's okay," he said again, "we don't mind that a bit!"

Sometime later I thanked Mrs. Phillips so much for their hospitality and the good meal, then said we had better get going. She looked at me with surprise, then said, "Surely your not going home today, we don't have many visitors and we thought you would stay for a day or two, anyway!"

Not only is the old-time cowboy gone, but so, too, is this entire type of people. The old-timers who lived an isolated life, whether in the Blackwater, the Rocky Mountain Trench or farther north, or any other area of northern Canada, were a completely different type of people. Just think about our day with the Phillips. We came completely by surprise, for the purpose of getting information from them. The oldest boy immediately stopped his work to entertain us. Pan stopped whatever he was doing to go and guide us in, and, at the least, we caused some problem with his horse, which still wasn't back when we left. I'm sure it also upset Mrs. Phillips' day, yet here they were, genuinely glad to see us and heartily inviting us back again, "To stay longer," as they said. Try driving your car or truck today into some strangers family ranching operation and see what your reception will be! My passenger didn't find himself any ranch land, but he was completely satisfied with the trip, saying it was a great day. I think he learned a thing or three about backwoods life on that trip, maybe he even learned something about flying in the hinterlands!

Shortly after I met Florence, the cute young lady who has now been my wife and constant companion for forty-some great years, I took her to the upper Blackwater. We flew to the abandoned Indian village on Kluskus Lake, where there is a fine old church. At least it was there at that time, and from what I understand, it may still be standing. We took pictures in the interior of the delicate religious figures and the pretty, colored windows with the sun shining through them. There was also a bell tower, complete with a big brass bell and a rope hanging down with which to ring the bell.

On the way out of the church I took hold of the rope, as if to pull it. "No, no," Florence said, "don't ring the bell."

"It's alright," I assured her, "there's no one close enough to hear it." Okay, so I wanted to impress my newly found girlfriend. I gave a few, even pulls on the rope. The melodious deep tones from the fine old bell rolled across the lake and over the surrounding hills, sounding hauntingly beautiful in the serene, picturesque wilderness setting, and it was even a Sunday!

An open, grassy hillside slopes up away from the lake and the buildings, topping more than a quarter-mile away. We walked out of the church, looked up the hillside and, lo and behold, there was an Indian on horseback, silhouetted on the ridge, crosswise to us and completely still like a statue! Really, one could just expect to see Roy Rogers come over the next knoll, riding Trigger!

Impress the girlfriend? Wow, I thought maybe I had just blown it. But all was well, the man on his horse didn't even come down to see us, and from time to time Florence and I still laugh about it, with her saying, "Yes, I was a bit nervous."

In 1972, after I had quit flying, moved from the area and went on to other ventures, our son Keith and I decided to go to the Blackwater. There was a trail, of sorts, to Kluskoil (Chinee) Lake, so we took with us bush-type motorbikes to navigate the swamps, creeks and rocks. Eventually, we stopped and could hear the noise from the falls on the river below the lake and I knew we were just about to reach the beautiful, pristine and remote spot on the isolated Chinee Lake of my memories.

How a once-great country can change so drastically in just a few short years, was painfully demonstrated to me in the next few minutes. There was now a lodge and cabins built on the formerly remote, baron, grassy lakeshore. A guide was bringing in U.S. fishermen with a high-clearance farm tractor pulling a rubber-tired, covered wagon. A woman was cooking at the lodge, clothes were drying on lines while people and dogs were coming and going from the cabins.

We walked to the river and discovered fishermen at the choice spots. I had built up Keith's expectations, telling him what the place used to be like. Quietly and sadly, we now looked for a spot, even a tiny bit remote, to set up our little tent. We brought just a fly rod and outfit along, to supply us with fat trout to cook over an open fire. We now had trouble catching even one fish for supper from my once great fishing river. It would have been okay if only we could have fished in one of the two or three choice holes. But these were all occupied by our American neighbors.

In the morning we discovered that one of the tourists would get up at daylight and go immediately to the best fishing hole. Later, his buddy would come and exchange places with him, so quickly that no one else could get in! They were using a baited hook with some weight to keep it down. With disgusting regularity a fish would take the bait. The "sportsman" would then reel in the fish, kill it, throw it on the bank and rebait the hook. When the partner came to change off, the one being relieved would take the fish with him. They kept virtually silent, not even exchanging words between themselves. The fishermen gave the appearance they were very reluctantly carrying out some chore that had to be done, showing the same amount of emotion or excitement that one would expect to see exhibited while washing his socks!

These great sportsmen fished the choice fishing hole constantly until dark, and this was during the long days of August. The next morning was a repeat of the previous day. What was even more sickening was to learn the guide, a local person, supposedly licensed, was taking all these excess fish and smoking them, making no attempt to stop the game hogs from taking many times more fish than they were legally entitled to. I have no idea how many fish they had caught and smoked, but we saw several fairly large boxes packed solid with smoked trout!

One day while we were away from our tent, a dog from camp got in and took our butter. I marched right up to the lodge and told the man there what had happened, and very sharply stated, "And I want a pound of butter." He gave us the butter, then invited us to supper with them that evening. I hated to, but the sight of all the choice food at the lodge influenced the decision for us and I accepted. At the table I was sitting next to a young man from Seattle. He almost immediately started telling us a story about strange and weird happenings in the nearby bush, which I had heard some twenty years previous. Originally, it probably had a ring of truth to it. It was about four quarters of a butchered moose being taken from a meat pole, without trace of where it went or what took it. A grizzly bear can easily take off with one quarter of moose, and maybe a persistent bear had taken all four.

But the story had now increased to a completely unbelievable state, with the young tourist telling about moose and other things disappearing, and huge, humanlike footprints sunk deep into the soil. The story was obviously intended to scare Keith and I, since we were sleeping in our little tent. Every one else at the table was quiet and when the yarn finally ended, the story teller looked at me for the "ohs and ahs" I would surely burst forth with. I looked at the person across the table from me and uttered one thing. I said, "Pass me the butter." The sad part was that the storyteller was so dumb, he didn't even know I had snubbed him!

Many times from the air, I had seen the rows of round depressions in the grassy soil on the flat above the river, indicating an ancient Native settlement. During the years I saw them, they were never disturbed. Now, one of the great fishermen told his guide, "Tomorrow, let's go and get those Indian artifacts." And their guide readily agreed to take them! I later asked the wife where the Indian relics were, just to see if it was where I thought they would be going, but she completely refused to talk to me.

When Keith and I left home on our trip to the Blackwater, we had a truck and camper, with the two trailbikes on a trailer behind the truck. Nearing the Blackwater area, we drove a little past Nazko village, where we parked the truck and camper off the trail in a clearing, while we had dinner and spent some leisure time.

Soon a team of horses and wagon came along, driven by an elderly Native, with a young girl riding on the wagon with him. He stopped his horses and asked where we were going. I told him, "We are going to try to get to Chinee Lake." I saw the slight change of expression on his face when I called the lake by their name, then he said, "I don't think you're going to make it with that outfit." He hadn't seen our motorbikes and thought I was going to try to get there with the camper. When I showed him the bikes, he grinned and thought that was a much better idea.

I told him I used to know the country fairly well, then I started inquiring about some of the people that I used to know. I asked about Mr. Charleyboy and he answered that he had died. I said he used to have a little girl living with him. He perked up, pointed to the girl on his wagon and said, "That was this girl's Mommy! She's in Nazko now," he continued. We talked some more, with him now talking very freely, when he saw that I knew the country and had known some of his people.

Finally, after the usual period of silence, he looked right at me and clearly stated, "These young Indians are no good!"

It took me so by surprise that I didn't know what to say. Finally, I blurted out, "Aren't they?"

"No," he said, "they lie, they steal, they won't work, you can't trust them; they're NO good."

"Gee, that's sure too bad."

"Yes," he said, "sure is too bad."

It gave me a very strange feeling. I felt awed, I felt humble to think that I had so gained the man's trust that he would talk to me like this. The old-time Indians of the Blackwater country that I knew were completely, 100 percent trustworthy. Remember how Mr. Charleyboy had felt so terrible to think that gas that I had left near his house had been stolen, and he couldn't stop it.

As they were about to start for Nazko, I told them about the Easter basket I had long ago brought for the little girl, and I asked the girl on the wagon to ask her Mommy if she remembered the Easter basket. They left for Nazko, which was close, and said they would soon be coming back.

About an hour later we heard the wagon coming. We were now in a clearing, about a hundred paces back from the road. As soon as the wagon came within sight of us, the same two occupants, the elderly man and the little girl, started waving vigorously. And of course we waved back. They kept up the hearty waving constantly, until they were out of sight, which must have taken three minutes!

Mommy had remembered the Easter basket! And as the two Natives, the elderly man and the little girl, disappeared from sight and the rattle of the wagon faded from earshot, I knew I was once again seeing the end of an era. How many times in my life must I witness the end of some grand period of history?

Epilogue

Before being married I enjoyed flying to some remote spot in the wilderness for days at a time. I also thought little about the hazards associated with the type of flying I was doing, although I knew full well the hazards were there. This knowledge was reinforced when a friend of mine who was a life insurance salesman told me there was no use in him trying to sell me life insurance because his company wouldn't insure me as long as I was doing this type of commercial flying!

After I was married my thoughts began to change and I began thinking more about things that could go wrong. This must have really been on my mind, because one night in a sound sleep I jumped out of bed, went to a window, pushed the curtain aside and tried to see what the weather was like—that was when Florence wakened me! One morning I was to take a BC Forest Service ranger on a low-level inspection trip with a wheel-equipped aircraft in a very mountainous area; we were checking to see if a lightning storm the previous evening had left any smoldering fires. As I was leaving the house Keith, our young son who was barely talking said to me the simple, "Bye, Dad."

After about two hours of flying, a weather front moved in, threatening to trap us behind a mountain range with no where to make a safe landing. All I could think of was that little boy with a happy look on his face as he waved goodbye to me. I wasn't being fair to my family and it was time to quit flying. We eventually left Prince George and moved to Salmon Arm, a nice town in a very pleasant area, where I went into the real estate business.

The flooding from the Peace River dam created a lake some 200 miles long from north to south, with a reach extending nearly 100 miles east to the dam. Along with all the beautiful and historic land flooded were the two old trading posts, Finlay Forks and Graham. The country was drastically changed forever. The logging firms moved in and built a network of roads that now cover much of the once-remote north, including a road to Fort Ware. However, those of us who have seen Ware as it used to be would not recognize it today. The government has built a large, modern school, with complete staff supplied from "down south." Also built were water and sewer systems, while a big diesel-powered generating station was installed. An airstrip was built, along with modern houses, complete with oil heat for all the residents at Ware. The Natives have contracted out their timber to the logging companies that have turned a forest that once had no end, even when viewed from the air, into what has been said to be the largest clearcut in B.C.

A friend of mine has worked in the carpentry field, off and on, for years at Ware and knows the Natives very well. He recently told me he was talking to quite an elderly Native at Ware, who told him in a subdued voice, "We liked it better the way it used to be, when we lived in our log cabins by the river!" I, too, liked it better the way it used to be.

Bibliography

Books cited

Bowes, Gordon E. editor, *Peace River Chronicles*, Prescott
    Publishing Company.

Condit, John, *Wings Over the West*, Harbour Publishing.

Hobson, Rich, *Grass Beyond the Mountains*, J. B. Lippincott
    Company.

Keith, Ronald A., *Bush Pilot with a Briefcase*, Doubleday Can.

Molson, K. M., *Pioneering in Canadian Air Transport*, W. D.
    Friesen & Sons, Publishers.

Patterson, R. M. *Finlay's River*, MacMillan Canada.

Other information sources

Canadian Aviation Magazine, Maclean-Hunter Publishers

Canadian National Aviation Museum

Aviation Museum in Winnipeg

Index

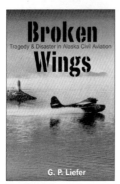

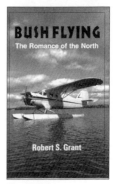

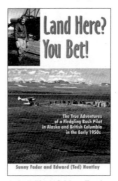

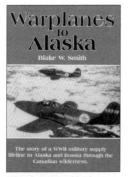
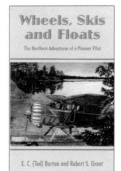
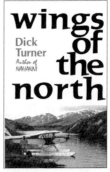